Boone Before Boone

Contributions to Southern Appalachian Studies

1. *Memoirs of Grassy Creek: Growing Up in the Mountains on the Virginia–North Carolina Line.* Zetta Barker Hamby. 1998
2. *The Pond Mountain Chronicle: Self-Portrait of a Southern Appalachian Community.* Edited by Leland R. Cooper and Mary Lee Cooper. 1998
3. *Traditional Musicians of the Central Blue Ridge: Old Time, Early Country, Folk and Bluegrass Label Recording Artists, with Discographies.* Marty McGee. 2000
4. *W.R. Trivett, Appalachian Pictureman: Photographs of a Bygone Time.* Ralph E. Lentz II. 2001
5. *The People of the New River: Oral Histories from the Ashe, Alleghany and Watauga Counties of North Carolina.* Edited by Leland R. Cooper and Mary Lee Cooper. 2001
6. *John Fox, Jr., Appalachian Author.* Bill York. 2003
7. *The Thistle and the Brier: Historical Links and Cultural Parallels Between Scotland and Appalachia.* Richard Blaustein. 2003
8. *Tales from Sacred Wind: Coming of Age in Appalachia. The Cratis Williams Chronicles.* Cratis D. Williams. Edited by David Cratis Williams and Patricia D. Beaver. 2003
9. *Willard Gayheart, Appalachian Artist.* Willard Gayheart and Donia S. Eley. 2003
10. *The Forest City Lynching of 1900: Populism, Racism, and White Supremacy in Rutherford County, North Carolina.* J. Timothy Cole. 2003
11. *The Brevard Rosenwald School: Black Education and Community Building in a Southern Appalachian Town, 1920–1966.* Betty J. Reed. 2004
12. *The Bristol Sessions: Writings About the Big Bang of Country Music.* Edited by Charles K. Wolfe and Ted Olson. 2005
13. *Community and Change in the North Carolina Mountains: Oral Histories and Profiles of People from Western Watauga County.* Compiled by Nannie Greene and Catherine Stokes Sheppard. 2006
14. *Ashe County: A History; A New Edition.* Arthur Lloyd Fletcher. 2009 [2006]
15. *The New River Controversy; A New Edition.* Thomas J. Schoenbaum. Epilogue by R. Seth Woodard. 2007
16. *The Blue Ridge Parkway by Foot: A Park Ranger's Memoir.* Tim Pegram. 2007
17. *James Still: Critical Essays on the Dean of Appalachian Literature.* Edited by Ted Olson and Kathy H. Olson. 2008
18. *Owsley County, Kentucky, and the Perpetuation of Poverty.* John R. Burch, Jr. 2008
19. *Asheville: A History.* Nan K. Chase. 2007
20. *Southern Appalachian Poetry: An Anthology of Works by 37 Poets.* Edited by Marita Garin. 2008
21. *Ball, Bat and Bitumen: A History of Coalfield Baseball in the Appalachian South.* L.M. Sutter. 2009
22. *The Frontier Nursing Service: America's First Rural Nurse-Midwife Service and School.* Marie Bartlett. 2009
23. *James Still in Interviews, Oral Histories and Memoirs.* Edited by Ted Olson. 2009
24. *The Millstone Quarries of Powell County, Kentucky.* Charles D. Hockensmith. 2009
25. *The Bibliography of Appalachia: More Than 4,700 Books, Articles, Monographs and Dissertations, Topically Arranged and Indexed.* Compiled by John R. Burch, Jr. 2009

26. *Appalachian Children's Literature: An Annotated Bibliography.* Compiled by Roberta Teague Herrin and Sheila Quinn Oliver. 2010

27. *Southern Appalachian Storytellers: Interviews with Sixteen Keepers of the Oral Tradition.* Edited by Saundra Gerrell Kelley. 2010

28. *Southern West Virginia and the Struggle for Modernity.* Christopher Dorsey. 2011

29. *George Scarbrough, Appalachian Poet: A Biographical and Literary Study with Unpublished Writings.* Randy Mackin. 2011

30. *The Water-Powered Mills of Floyd County, Virginia: Illustrated Histories, 1770–2010.* Franklin F. Webb and Ricky L. Cox. 2012

31. *School Segregation in Western North Carolina: A History, 1860s–1970s.* Betty Jamerson Reed. 2011

32. *The Ravenscroft School in Asheville: A History of the Institution and Its People and Buildings.* Dale Wayne Slusser. 2014

33. *The Ore Knob Mine Murders: The Crimes, the Investigation and the Trials.* Rose M. Haynes. 2013

34. *New Art of Willard Gayheart.* Willard Gayheart and Donia S. Eley. 2014

35. *Public Health in Appalachia: Essays from the Clinic and the Field.* Edited by Wendy Welch. 2014

36. *The Rhetoric of Appalachian Identity.* Todd Snyder. 2014

37. *African American and Cherokee Nurses in Appalachia: A History, 1900–1965.* Phoebe Ann Pollitt. 2016

38. *A Hospital for Ashe County: Four Generations of Appalachian Community Health Care.* Janet C. Pittard. 2016

39. *Dwight Diller: West Virginia Mountain Musician.* Lewis M. Stern. 2016

40. *The Brown Mountain Lights: History, Science and Human Nature Explain an Appalachian Mystery.* Wade Edward Speer. 2017

41. *Richard L. Davis and the Color Line in Ohio Coal: A Hocking Valley Mine Labor Organizer, 1862–1900.* Frans H. Doppen. 2016

42. *The Silent Appalachian: Wordless Mountaineers in Fiction, Film and Television.* Vicki Sigmon Collins. 2017

43. *The Trees of Ashe County, North Carolina.* Doug Munroe. 2017

44. *Melungeon Portraits: Exploring Kinship and Identity.* Tamara L. Stachowicz. 2018

45. *Always Been a Rambler: G.B. Grayson and Henry Whitter, Country Music Pioneers of Southern Appalachia.* Josh Beckworth. 2018

46. *Tommy Thompson: New-Timey String Band Musician.* Lewis M. Stern. 2019

47. *Appalachian Fiddler Albert Hash: The Last Leaf on the Tree.* Malcolm L. Smith with Edwin Lacy. 2020

48. *Junaluska: Oral Histories of a Black Appalachian Community.* Edited by Susan E. Keefe with the Junaluska Heritage Association. 2020

49. *Boone Before Boone: The Archaeological Record of Northwestern North Carolina Through 1769.* Tom Whyte. 2020

50. *From the Front Lines of the Appalachian Addiction Crisis: Healthcare Providers Discuss Opioids, Meth and Recovery.* Edited by Wendy Welch. 2020

51. *Writers by the River: Reflections on 40+ Years of the Highland Summer Conference.* Edited by Donia S. Eley and Grace Toney Edwards. 2020

52. *Wayne Howard: Old Time Music, the Hammons Family and Mountain Lore.* Lewis M. Stern. 2021

Boone Before Boone

The Archaeological Record of Northwestern North Carolina Through 1769

Tom Whyte

Contributions to
Southern Appalachian Studies, 49

McFarland & Company, Inc., Publishers
Jefferson, North Carolina

LIBRARY OF CONGRESS CATALOGUING-IN-PUBLICATION DATA

Names: Whyte, Thomas R., author.
Title: Boone before Boone : the archaeological record of northwestern North Carolina through 1769 / Tom Whyte.
Other titles: Contributions to southern Appalachian studies ; 49.
Description: Jefferson, North Carolina : McFarland & Company, Inc., Publishers, 2020 | Series: Contributions to southern Appalachian studies; 49 | Includes bibliographical references and index.
Identifiers: LCCN 2020042655 | ISBN 9781476683423 (paperback : acid free paper) ∞
ISBN 9781476641362 (ebook)
Subjects: LCSH: Indians of North America—North Carolina, Western—Antiquities. | North Carolina, Western—Antiquities.
Classification: LCC E78.N74 W53 2020 | DDC 975.6/01—dc23
LC record available at https://lccn.loc.gov/2020042655

BRITISH LIBRARY CATALOGUING DATA ARE AVAILABLE

ISBN (print) 978-1-4766-8342-3
ISBN (ebook) 978-1-4766-4136-2

© 2020 Tom Whyte. All rights reserved

No part of this book may be reproduced or transmitted in any form or by any means, electronic or mechanical, including photocopying or recording, or by any information storage and retrieval system, without permission in writing from the publisher.

On the cover: author's rendition of Native Appalachian life, circa 1300 CE (courtesy of the Frank H. McClung Museum of Natural History & Culture, University of Tennessee, Knoxville); *background* Boone in late fall © 2020 Ian Brundige/Shutterstock

Printed in the United States of America

McFarland & Company, Inc., Publishers
Box 611, Jefferson, North Carolina 28640
www.mcfarlandpub.com

To the memory of
Norman Dean Jefferson,
1952–1999

Photograph by Rob Hunter.

Table of Contents

Acknowledgments — x

Preface — 1

Introduction — 3

1. Paleoindian Period: 11,500–9,500 BCE — 17
2. Early Archaic Period: 8,000–6,000 BCE — 38
3. Middle Archaic Period: 6,000–3,000 BCE — 57
4. Late Archaic Period: 3,000 to 1,000 BCE — 75
5. Early Woodland Period: 1,000 BCE–200 CE — 96
6. Middle Woodland Period: 200–900 CE — 112
7. Late Woodland Period: 900–1400 CE — 128
8. Contact: Late May 1540 CE — 153

Conclusion — 159

Bibliography — 161

Index — 173

Acknowledgments

Many great archaeologists, including my current and former colleagues, professors, and professional peers, have inspired me. These include Harvard Ayers, Cliff Boyd, Donna Boyd, Bill Boyer, Jeff Chapman, Cheryl Claassen, Steve Davis, Roy Dickens, Charles Faulkner, Clarence Geier, Cameron Gokee, Joe Herbert, Norman Jefferson, Bennie Keel, Larry Kimball, Walter Klippel, Maureen Meyers, David Moore, Carole Nash, Paul Parmalee, Burt Purrington, Brett Riggs, Gerald Schroedl, Sarah Sherwood, Ben Steere, Steve Thompson, Trawick Ward, and Alice Wright. Of these, I am especially indebted to Larry Kimball, the smartest archaeologist I have ever known. Many avocational archaeologists and landowners also have been very generous with their knowledge and access to sites on their properties. Of these, I am especially indebted to Cecil Ward, Diane Price, Rob Griffith, Margot Birckhead, Annabel Harrill, and Charles Church. I have benefited from the support of the Appalachian State University Department of Anthropology and the College of Arts and Sciences. I thank Christopher R. Moore for my base maps. My most heartfelt thanks are for my family—Lauri, Alice, and Sadie Whyte. They are my bright lights.

Preface

I have been doing archaeology in the southern Appalachian region for over forty years. Most of my research and that of my colleagues has resulted in technical reports, articles, book chapters, and conference papers that are read almost exclusively by professional archaeologists. This book is an opportunity to summarize the discoveries and interpretations of archaeological evidence of Native American life in northwestern North Carolina in a package that can be readily gotten and enjoyed by anyone. In writing this book I have attempted to find a middle road between scholarship and public education. In so doing I have avoided disciplinary jargon and glossed over many tedious details of the findings and interpretations of archaeology to create something that might be enjoyed by any reader with an interest in western North Carolina's ancient human past. Each chapter provides an overview of archaeological evidence and interpretations of precontact (before the European invasions) Native American life for a major time division traditionally recognized by archaeologists working in the region. The divisions between these periods are not random, but rather have been defined by changes in material culture such as spear point shapes or the appearance of pottery. Many of these changes in material culture came about because of changes in climate, human settlement, or socio-political complexity. I begin each chapter with a fictional narrative in an attempt to "flesh out" Native American life in the Appalachian Summit at the time. These stories, albeit based on archaeological evidence, are only stories. I am not a Native American and cannot pretend to have the spiritual, cultural, or imaginative tools to take the reader back into the Native American past. My goal is simply to give some life to the inert facts of science.

Also, in each chapter I cite the evidence from one or two archaeological sites to tell a story of human life in Appalachian Summit precontact times. Many of the sites chosen as examples are ones that I or my

Preface

close colleagues have researched and with which I am very familiar, and most of them are very close to (and some are in) Boone, North Carolina. It will be evident to the reader that we know a great deal more about more recent times than we do the shadowy ancient ones. This is largely because more materials, especially organic remains such as food refuse, implements and tools of wood, bone, and plant fiber, and the skeletal remains of the humans themselves are better preserved on the more recent sites. The contexts (deposits and spatial juxtapositions of artifacts, etc.) on those sites also are better preserved. It also is the case that there has been more archaeological research focused on the more recent sites, in part, *because* of the excellent preservation they afford.

In this text I have chosen to present dates with reference to the "Common Era" (BCE is equivalent to BC and CE is equivalent to AD) rather than with reference to the birth of one particular religious figure. "Years before present" (YBP) also is a problematic reference, as future readers of the text are in a different "present." A reader may add the current calendrical year to a date presented as BCE to determine the number of years lapsed (YBP) since the date of the artifact, site, or event discussed. I also use the metric system for all measurements except for altitudes. This is generally the convention for the sciences in the United States.

A final note is that archaeology is a very dynamic but young science. New discoveries, being made every day, sometimes disprove previous interpretations and open doors for new questions. For example, only 30 years ago it was thought by most researchers that no humans had been in the Americas until about 13,000 years ago. We have now doubled that number! Only within the last ten years did we discover that modern humans had mated with Neandertals and Denisovans, and the origin of our species has been pushed back another 100,000 years. Archaeology also is a science in which there is much disagreement. In this book I have tried to present the opinions of the wider field rather than to promote my own (some of which may seem outlandish!). My sincere hope is that the reader will become enlightened but remain inquisitive and excited about discoveries yet to be made.

Introduction

On May 21, 1540, when Hernando de Soto with his 600 men, 300 horses, herd of pigs, and fierce mastiffs marched into the village of Xuala along the Catawba River in Burke County, North Carolina, he did not know nor did he care that the native residents, whom he was about to change forever, were human beings with a rich and very deep cultural heritage. His goal was to discover gold. At that time, Europeans were unaware of the depth of their *own* cultural heritage beyond what was, to them, clearly chronicled by the Judeo-Christian Book of Genesis. There was no concept of a "pre" history. All of human existence was neatly packaged in the Old Testament and other writings. For some of us the idea of humans existing anywhere prior to 5,000 or 6,000 years ago is difficult to grasp. Yet fossil and archaeological evidence has shown that humans (genus *Homo*) have existed for about 3,000,000 (three million) years. Our own species, *Homo sapiens*, has existed for about 300,000 years and, in our gradual spread from Africa, made it to eastern North America by as early as 18,000 years ago.

Often, visitors to my archaeological excavations, which may be on a site that dates to 7,000 years ago, will ask: "what kind of Indians were they?" I know they expect me to answer "Cherokee," but the fact is, with reference to pre-contact (before Europeans) humans, we cannot know what they called themselves. There were no Cherokee, Catawba, or even English, Hindi, Mandarin, or Swahili speakers 7,000 years ago. Most of us have no knowledge of the vast and deep history of the native people of the southern Appalachian region before the time of Daniel Boone. The people had no need for writing and only some of their oral histories have survived. The evidence of most of their existence lies in the archaeological record—the places they occupied and the scantly preserved remains of their structures, artifacts, food refuse, and skeletons. Yet people have been in these mountains since before the end of the Ice Age, over 13,000

Introduction

years ago. In those 13,000 years there have been many languages, religions, and ways of life.

In 1540, when de Soto passed through western North Carolina, the Cherokees occupied much of southwestern North Carolina, northern Georgia, and eastern Tennessee. The Cherokees speak an Iroquoian language dialect related to the other Iroquoian dialects of the historic tribes of Pennsylvania, New York, and southern Ontario. The eastern foothills of the Blue Ridge, at the headwaters of the Catawba and Yadkin rivers, were occupied mostly by speakers of a Siouan language, including various ancestral tribes of today's Catawbas.

The de Soto entrada was the first European invasion of the Southern Appalachians. Over the subsequent 300 years or so, other Spanish, English, and even Moravian visitors, and Daniel Boone, would follow. When the Moravian, August Gottlieb Spangenberg, arrived in the mountains near present-day Boone, North Carolina, in December 1752, he observed no humans or evidence of them as he surveyed the highlands for Moravian land claims. Spangenberg arrived in early winter when the natives that may have passed through in the fall while hunting deer and gathering nuts were safely encamped in the warmer lowlands to the east and west. This was the time of the Little Ice Age, a period of slightly cooler weather that lasted from 1400 to 1850 CE; there were no permanent residents in the higher elevations of the region at that time. Because of the truncated growing season, they would not have been able to grow, harvest, and store enough food to get them through winter.

And then came Daniel Boone in 1769, often romanticized as the wilderness explorer who made it possible for European Americans to conquer the west by leading about 50 people, along with his family, through Cumberland Gap into what is now Kentucky. They probably encountered little or no resistance as they wound their way along the trails through the mountains. Native Americans and their large mammalian prey such as deer, elk, and in the late Ice Age, woodlands caribou and peccaries probably blazed these ancient trails. Despite popular accounts, there is no evidence that the American bison or "buffalo" was in the southern Appalachian Mountain region until after 1700, yet there has been a tendency to call the trails "buffalo trails" (Ward 1990).

Archaeologists refer to the higher elevations of the southern Appalachian region as the "Appalachian Summit" (Kroeber 1939). This includes the southern portion of the Blue Ridge physiographic province of the Appalachian Mountain chain and has a geography and cultural history that distinguish it from the rest of the adjacent highlands. Today

Introduction

it is known as the homeland of the Cherokees but is shared by diverse immigrants from all continents. It is also the heart of "Appalachia" and the place of "Appalachian Culture," a distinctive characterization of human life and mountain adaptation developing out of European/African American colonization of the region. This culture expresses a blending of heritages with many families claiming (and some, rightfully so) some degree of Cherokee ancestry.

The name "Appalachian" comes from an early sixteenth century Spanish record of a Native American town "Apalchen" near Tallahassee, Florida. The residents of the town were later called the "Apalachee Indians." The Spanish then decided to name the mountains to the north of this region, where they intended to search for gold, the "Appalachian Mountains." The proper pronunciation, therefore, much to the dismay of modern-day visitors from the north and elsewhere, is with a soft a before the c; it is not a homophone for "appellation."

The region includes portions of southwestern Virginia, eastern Tennessee, western North Carolina, northeastern Georgia, and northwestern South Carolina in elevation above 1,500 feet above mean sea level (Figure I.1). The rugged, seemingly random topography, stands in contrast to the gentler, more linear ranges of the Valley and Ridge (VRP) province to the west and north. This topographic confusion is, in part, a result of the dissection of the region by river system headwaters flowing to the east (Yadkin and Catawba rivers), the south (Saluda, Keowee, Chattooga, and Chattahoochee), the west (Little Tennessee, Watauga, Holston, French Broad) and north (New) (Figure I.1). The convergence of these headwaters in the Appalachian Summit played an important role in human settlement and commerce throughout precontact times. The rich resources sought by ancient humans in the Appalachian Summit include soapstone for the making of cooking vessels; mica used in works of art and religious paraphernalia; nuts from the oak, hickory, and chestnut forests; a great abundance of fish and game; and parts of the landscape itself that provided shelter, burial places, and connections with the spirit world. But the abundance and variety of food seems to have drawn more visitors to the region than any other prospect.

Archaeologists working in the region for over 100 years have begun to flesh out the lives of the ancient predecessors of today's native mountain residents. The first archaeological investigations, sponsored by the Bureau of American Ethnology (BAE) of the Smithsonian Institution from 1882 to 1886, focused on earthen mounds that the Native Americans had long ago constructed for ritual purposes. The mound

Introduction

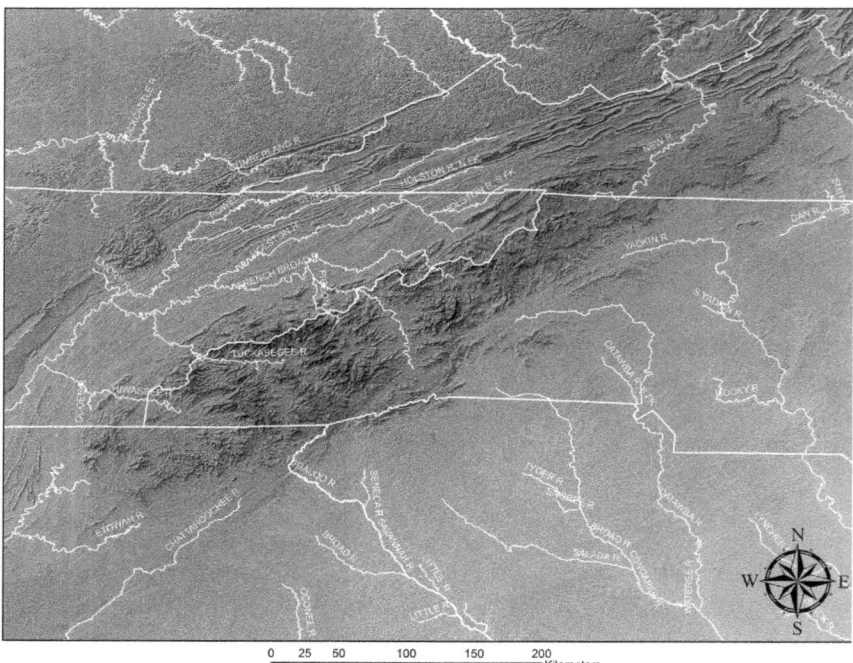

Figure I.1. The Appalachian Summit Region.

explorations of the BAE in North Carolina focused on mound and burial sites in Buncombe, Burke, Caldwell, Haywood, Henderson, and Wilkes Counties (Thomas 1985). Mounds are relatively rare in western North Carolina. Some, however, such as the Garden Creek Mounds in Haywood County, Biltmore Mound in Buncombe County, Peachtree Mound in Cherokee County, and Nikwasi Mound in Macon County have played important roles in the history of archaeology in North Carolina and have provided many insights into the region's native human past. Only a few of these mounds, including Nikwasi Mound (Figure I.2), remain relatively intact.

In 1933 and 1934 the Civil Works Administration of the U.S. government sponsored excavations at Peachtree Mound and Village site in Cherokee County, North Carolina (Setzler and Jennings 1941). At that same time, Joffre L. Coe, a young man from Greensboro, North Carolina, became involved in the state's archaeological society and formulated a plan to initiate a statewide survey that included the mountainous western region (Ward and Davis 1999). Archaeological investigations

Introduction

Figure I.2. Nikwasi Mound in Franklin, North Carolina (courtesy of the Research Laboratories of Archaeology, University of North Carolina at Chapel Hill).

in the mountains, however, did not commence until the 1960s when Coe, then armed with a Ph.D. and ensconced at the University of North Carolina at Chapel Hill, formulated the Cherokee Project. This led to extensive surveys in the southwestern counties and excavations at the Tuckasegee site in Jackson County, the Townson site in Cherokee County, the Garden Creek site in Haywood County, and the Warren Wilson site in Buncombe County.

It was through these projects that much of the nomenclature and cultural history of western North Carolina archaeology was defined. Unfortunately, it was defined for *southwestern* North Carolina where the investigations were focused, but was feebly applied to findings from the northwestern mountains of the state in subsequent decades by newly transplanted archaeologists. Appalachian State University (ASU) began its program of archaeological investigations in the northwestern counties, primarily Watauga and Ashe, in 1971. The new archaeologists, Burton L. Purrington and Harvard G. Ayers, were to discover that the archaeological record of much of the Native American past of this region, especially that of later precontact times, differed significantly from that in the southwestern part of the state. From 1971 to the present, ASU archaeology has dominated the research of the northwestern

Introduction

counties, conducting extensive surveys of the Watauga and New River valleys and numerous excavations of sites of all periods. Most of the evidence discussed in the following chapters resulted from this work.

Thousands of Native American archaeological sites have been discovered in northwestern North Carolina. This is only a small sample of what once existed, and probably thousands remain to be discovered. Most of them are small, temporary campsites containing a smattering of stone artifacts and maybe some pottery fragments. Yet these sites are important sources of information about the ancient people of the region just as pyramids and tombs are in Egypt and Mesoamerica. When people learn that I am an archaeologist, they often ask me if I travel to Egypt or the Middle East to do fieldwork. My reply is that I rarely excavate beyond 50 kilometers of Boone. The mysteries of the human past of the North Carolina mountains are no less intriguing.

A Brief Overview of Archaeology

Archaeology is the study of undocumented evidence of the human past. This evidence consists of human remains, archaeological sites, artifacts, remains of structures, cultural features such as hearths, mounds, and food storage pits, and human refuse such as animal bones and plant remains. This differentiates archaeology from history—the study of the documented and oral records of the human past; although the goals are similar, the sources of evidence are different. Because no writing existed anywhere prior to about 3,400 BCE, and our genus (*Homo*) has been around for approximately 3,000,000 years, most of what we know about the human past has come to light through archaeology and human paleontology (the study of ancient human skeletal remains). In fact, much of what we know about the historical period (that which has been documented to some extent) has been learned through archaeology. Historical writings tend to focus on economic and political events, whereas the quotidian details of everyday human life are found in and on the ground—in the archaeological record.

The goals of archaeology are to discover evidence of the human past, preserve that evidence, determine what human life was like at any time or place in the past, and explain the temporal and geographic variation in past human lifeways and adaptations. Evidence of the human past is better preserved in some places and contexts than others. This

Introduction

is especially the case for organic remains, seldom preserved on more ancient sites. Arid regions and dry caves are especially beneficial for preservation of organic remains such as human tissues and food refuse because micro-organisms and insects that would normally consume organic tissues are less active in the absence of moisture or warm temperatures. Examples include the naturally mummified humans who were buried over 5,000 years ago in the Xinjiang Province of arid western China (Discover 1994). Their clothing, hair, and skin remain remarkably intact. Excavations in Lovelock Cave, in the dry Great Basin desert region of Nevada, yielded grass sandals, duck decoys and thousands of human feces, some dated to over 10,000 years ago (Heizer and Napton 1970). Very cold climates, similarly, are good for the preservation of organic tissues. This is why we freeze and refrigerate our foods. The Ice man known as Ötzi, found thawing out of ice and snow in the Tyrolean Alps of northern Italy in 1991, was at first thought to be a recently deceased skier or mountaineer—until they found his stone knife, copper axe and woven grass cape. He was murdered in the Alps over 5,000 years ago (Fleckinger 2018). Anaerobic (low oxygen) settings, such as waterlogged ground and peat bogs, for the same reason, are good places for organic preservation. For example, the well-known bog mummies of northern Europe are incredibly well preserved because of the anaerobic and tannin-rich environment in which they were deposited thousands of years ago (Aldhouse-Green 2015).

Calcium-rich soils such as those of the Valley and Ridge Province, just west of the Appalachian Summit, are conducive to preservation of bone and shell because the calcium that comprises much of the mineralogy of bone and shell is bolstered and stabilized by calcium in the soil. In contrast, the calcium in bone and shell deposited in acidic soils leaches out, thus destabilizing the structure of the object. A primary reason for the amazing preservation of bones of extinct Pliocene (4,900,000 to 4,700,000-year-old) fauna at the Gray Fossil site in Washington County, Tennessee, is that the remains accumulated in a calcium-rich limestone sinkhole.

Deep and rapid burial of archaeological remains is conducive to their preservation and to the stabilization of their contexts. This shields them from movement and degradation by surface processes such as weathering, animal and insect burrowing, tree roots, cultivation, and the like.

Pompeii and Herculaneum in Italy, quickly buried by volcanic ash, are cases in point. This is one reason why archaeologists focus much

Introduction

attention on deeply buried, stratified sites. The materials and contexts, better preserved, are analogous to modern crime scenes in which all of the evidence is left in place; when evidence is moved or taken away, the crime is much more difficult to reconstruct. Moreover, stratified sites—ones that contain sequential layers of evidence of ancient human life—provide opportunities to study human cultural and biological change through time within a specific region. Sadly, most archaeological sites are located immediately below the surface and in environments that are not ideal for preservation of materials and contexts. Consequently, most have been disturbed or destroyed, and those that remain contain only the most durable objects of stone, ceramic, or metal that have survived the ravages of time. It is, in part, because of this that archaeology has become somewhat of a forensic science.

Finding Archaeological Sites

Many archaeological sites, such as Stonehenge in England and the Pyramids of Egypt, have never been lost. Others, previously lost below flood deposits, through sea-level rise, or beneath jungle growth have been discovered by accident. But most have to be sought through systematic archaeological survey methods. One of the easiest ways that archaeologists find terrestrial sites is to simply walk across the surface of the ground in search of evidence of past human activity—things such as artifacts, human bones, and structural remains. This technique, sometimes called "surface survey" or "pedestrian survey," is only effective in discovering surface sites and in areas where there is surface visibility such as recently plowed fields or desert margins. When evidence is found, it is often collected and mapped to reveal the spatial extent of the site. Sites of all ages and types have been found using this method.

In areas where the ground is covered with grass or other vegetation, archaeologists often undertake systematic interval testing of the ground by digging small pits (30–50 cm) with shovels at evenly spaced grid intervals (perhaps 10 or 20 m) across the landscape. The soil from each pit is then screened to recover artifacts or other evidence indicating the presence of a site. Although this method is effective in vegetated areas, it still only "scratches the surface" in that the pits can be excavated only so deep; many archaeological sites are buried several meters below the surface.

Deeply buried archeological sites, unless they are exposed in an eroding riverbank, shoreline, or road-cut, can only be found by digging

Introduction

deep pits or trenches, sometimes using a backhoe, to expose the evidence in a trench profile. This is a highly destructive method, but a small sacrifice for the reward of finding these buried, often well-preserved and ancient sites that would otherwise remain undiscovered.

There also are noninvasive geophysical methods for locating archaeological evidence, but they are seldom used to look for previously undiscovered sites. Rather, they are used to detect specific kinds of evidence such as graves and structural remains on sites that have already been identified. These include ground penetrating radar, magnetometry, and resistivity. A ground penetrating radar device sends a radio wave into the ground that reflects from objects and soil density boundaries back to the device. Radar anomalies that vary from the general range of undisturbed areas of the site are detected and often form geometric shapes or clusters of shapes on the device's monitor, indicating the possible locations of structures, graves, etc.

Magnetometry works in much the same way but records variations in soil magnetism below the surface. Soil magnetism can be increased by the burning of structures, firing pottery, and by concentrating organic remains in midden areas. Iron objects are also detected by magnetometry. Resistivity employs a device that circulates an electrical current through the soil and back to the device. The current may be weakened if it passes through loose soil and remain stronger if it passes through compact or moist soil. These electrical anomalies, expressed as peaks and valleys on the device's monitor, may indicate where human activity has disturbed the ground. Regardless of which geophysical method is employed in the search for evidence of human activity, "ground-truthing" (verification through excavation) is required to determine what the detected anomalies are, and whether they are the results of human activity.

A final method of discovering archaeological evidence is by way of satellite imagery. Sometimes large archaeological sites such as towns, ceremonial centers, and enclosures are buried under dense jungle growth, just beneath desert sands, or in shallow coastal waters where they are difficult to recognize at close range, but readily visible from a great distance. For example, David Kennedy, a professor of classics and ancient history at the University of Western Australia, used Google Earth satellite maps to locate nearly 2,000 potential archaeological sites, including 1,082 teardrop-shaped stone tombs in arid regions of Saudi Arabia (Kennedy and Bishop 2011).

Introduction

Excavating Archaeological Sites

There are nearly as many ways to excavate a site as there are sites; every site is unique and requires a particular suite of techniques. How a site is to be taken apart depends on the questions to be answered by the research, the setting of the site, and the nature and contents of its matrix; caves and rockshelters require different methods and tools than open-air sites. Surface sites are altogether different from deeply stratified sites. Sites with amazing organic preservation and human remains require a different approach than ones containing only stone artifacts. In a typical terrestrial situation, archaeologists often impose a grid of squares on the surface of the site that will allow them to systematically dissect and sample the site and map the locations of found objects. Vertical excavation within these squares is subdivided by observable strata or, in their absence, arbitrary depth increments of perhaps a few centimeters. This allows the archaeologist to separate layers or deposits representing different episodes of human occupation. Special features such as structures, cellars, burials, and hearths require more specific excavation methods to document their configurations and recover their contents.

There are several ways of recovering material evidence during excavation. Some objects are observed while digging, their locations recorded on a map, and then gently removed by hand for transport back to the laboratory. Most objects, because of their small size, are not observed while digging but recovered when sediments are passed through a screen. When delicate organic objects such as animal bones and carbonized plant remains are present in the matrix, sediments will be processed by wet screening, which allows for the use of finer meshes, or by flotation, which gently floats plant remains and separates them from coarser objects and sediment.

The most important part of the process of archaeology is thorough documentation. No matter how carefully a site is taken apart, its contexts are effectively destroyed and cannot be put back together. The objects recovered can be preserved with proper curation; however, the excavated contexts can only be preserved in recorded forms such as maps, measurements, written descriptions, and photographs. Field archaeologists often spend more time holding a pencil or camera than a trowel or shovel. With proper documentation, excavated archaeological sites can continue to be researched long into the future as new questions and theories arise.

Introduction

Sadly, well-preserved archaeological evidence of the ancient human past is becoming scarce, primarily due to the impacts of our industries on the landscape—things such as road, house, shopping mall, and reservoir construction—but also because of artifact collecting. When artifacts are removed from their contexts and when sites are vandalized or destroyed by collectors or construction projects, the result is no different than the burning of a rare ancient text; information about the human past is lost forever. And no artifact in the Appalachian Summit is more prized among collectors than the Clovis spear point, possibly the earliest evidence of humans in these mountains.

How Archaeological Sites Are Dated

Until 1950 the ages of pre-contact sites in the Appalachian Summit could only be guessed. Archaeologists did their best to sort out artifacts and ancient cultures by observing changes in technologies and other evidence through time, especially by examining their relative vertical positions in stratified sites. These observations gave us much of the nomenclature that is still used today to describe time periods, artifact styles, and cultural groupings of the past, such as the "Archaic period" and the "Morrow Mountain phase." But the actual ages or time spans of these entities were not known. Now there are dozens of chronometric dating methods (ones that provide close estimates of age), two of which are commonly used in the Appalachian Summit region.

Carbon-14 dating, one of our most dependable methods, is based on the rate of radioactive decay of ^{14}C, a carbon isotope that is found in the atmosphere and all living organisms. The isotope, which has an unstable nucleus, is respired along with carbon dioxide by plants that are in turn consumed by animals and humans. When an organism dies, the ^{14}C molecules in its tissues randomly decay (by releasing a neutron from the nucleus) into Nitrogen 14 with a half-life of 5,730 years. In other words, after 5,730 years has lapsed since the death of a deer, a human, or a tree limb, roughly half of the ^{14}C relative to other carbon molecules in remaining tissues will have disappeared. After another 5,730 years, only a fourth will remain, and so on. After about 50,000 years has lapsed since the death of the organism there is no measurable ^{14}C left for the dating method to be used. This is not a problem for archaeologists working in the Americas; there were no humans here until much later.

This method, then requires a piece of something that was once alive (organic matter), and that the object be less than 50,000 years old. Quite

Introduction

often, small fragments of wood charcoal from an ancient hearth are all that remains of organic materials that had been deposited on a site. These are datable by the carbon-14 method because they are organic. When we date wood charcoal, we are determining when the wood died. Presumably, twigs and branches collected for firewood died not long before being used as fuel, and so the resulting date is a reasonable proxy for the age of site occupation and human activity. Other materials commonly dated include animal bones, human bones (but only with permission of native descendants), and carbonized organic residues adhering to fragments of cooking vessels.

When organic samples are selected for dating, the amount of ^{14}C remaining can be measured by a radiocarbon dating lab either directly by using accelerator mass spectrometry (AMS), or indirectly by using a Geiger counter, which measures the rate of radioactive decay. With either measurement method, the half-life is factored into the equation and an average of several measurements is calculated. This translates to a probable age with some degree of variance, such as "$3,130 \pm 30$ years before present."

When ^{14}C dates are obtained on organic materials associated with certain types of spear points or pottery, we can then use those types of artifacts as proxies for estimating the ages of archaeological sites. For example, if I find a site containing many pieces of Swannanoa cord-marked pottery on the surface, I can estimate that the site was occupied around 3,000 years ago, because organic materials found with this kind of pottery date to that time. Many sites in the Appalachian Summit have been typologically dated in this way. However, archaeologists must be cautious in estimating the age of a site's occupation on the basis of one artifact such as a Clovis spear point; many stone artifacts were scavenged, re-used, relocated, and discarded by later stone tool users (Whyte 2014).

Several sites discussed in this book were dated by the carbon-14 method, including Church Rockshelter No. 1, where porcupine bones and teeth, wood charcoal, and organic residues adhering to pottery indicated varying dates of site occupation. At the Gwyn Hayes site in Boone, wood charcoal from a hearth yielded a ^{14}C date of 2,110–2,090 BCE. Several ^{14}C dates were obtained on wood charcoal and pottery residues from the Katie Griffith site in northern Watauga County indicating a residence there at approximately 1350 CE.

Another chronometric dating method, only recently gaining regular use in the mountains, is optically stimulated luminescence (OSL)

Introduction

dating. This method can be conducted on alluvial (water-transported) or aeolian (windborne) sand grains from strata associated with archaeological evidence or on sand grains found in pottery. Molecules in quartz and feldspar grains that are protected from heat and sunlight, over time accumulate loosely bonded ionizing radiation at a relatively constant rate. Much like mold growing on bread, the longer it sits on the shelf (the longer the grains are protected from light or heat by being buried in the ground or within the wall of a ceramic vessel), the more mold that grows. Archaeologists recover soil samples from their strata without exposing them to sunlight and submit them to a dating lab, which measures the amount of loosely bonded ionizing radiation. This is equated to the amount of time that has passed since the grains were last exposed to sunlight—that is, when they were at the surface and when the site was occupied by humans. Subsequent burial of the sediments and archaeological remains by flood deposits, slope-wash, or aeolian sands, then, allowed them to begin accumulating the ionizing radiation that was measured in the lab.

In the case of OSL dating of pottery, quartz and feldspar grains trapped inside the ceramic body are protected from sunlight and, after they are broken and discarded, from heat. The lab measures the amount of ionizing radiation that these grains have accumulated since their last exposure to sunlight and heat and equates this measure to the amount of time lapsed. Early Woodland Swannanoa pottery from Church Rockshelter No. 2 in Watauga County, North Carolina, was OSL dated to approximately 1,080 BCE. Aeolian sand grains that accumulated around and on top of artifacts at the Cactus Hill site in eastern Virginia were OSL dated to approximately 17,000 years ago, making it one of the earliest archaeological sites in eastern North America (McAvoy and McAvoy 2015).

1

Paleoindian Period: 11,500–9,500 BCE

He had never seen a summer so warm and dry. It was the perfect chance to explore the mountains, secure some of the precious black flint that was known to exist in the rock formations and stream gravels just beyond, and for his daughter and two sons to find mates. Their mother had been killed by a saber-toothed tiger three years ago while foraging for edible fruits in the eastern foothills of the mountains. At other times of the year, and even in previous summers, the mountains were a formidable barrier. But the present warming made them more inviting. They would follow what would later be called the Yadkin River westward to its headwaters, travel through a gap into a high valley beyond the Blue Ridge, and then follow another river westward to the flint-bearing limestone formations of the big valley beyond. Between the headwaters of the Yadkin and Watauga, they would briefly encounter the north-flowing headwaters of the New River, where they would camp for a night.

The paths they would take were as old as the mountains themselves. They had been carved out by herds of Ice Age mammals that had preceded the humans and were maintained by the constant migrations of humans and fauna between the uplands and lowlands. Some of these paths would much later become trade routes, warpaths, wagon roads, and then four-lane highways such as NC Highway 321. Some would be erroneously labeled "buffalo trails" because of an occasional sighting of a buffalo by Euro-American frontiersmen like Daniel Boone.

In the mountains there were a few lingering caribou, horses, and peccaries, although their numbers were giving way to deer and elk more adapted to the expanding forests. His hunting grounds in the lowlands to the east were teeming with bison, wooly mammoths, mastodons, horses, and giant ground sloths. These were good to eat, but not as good or as easy to hunt and process as the deer and turkey. Furthermore, the bones, hides, and antlers of deer were much more suited to his various other needs.

Everything they owned they carried with them in woven bags tied around their necks or to their belts—their deerskin clothing and boots, woven bags containing bone, antler, and ivory tools, stone tool preforms for making new spear points, stone blades for cutting, scraping, planing, drilling, or sawing, scraps of sinew and braided twine, dried meats and berries for food, dried mushrooms and leaves for medicine, fire-starting equipment, a wooden bowl for gathering seeds, berries, and water, and animal hides for protection and comfort. Their portable tools, of necessity, were multifunctional; spear points were also knives, hide scrapers were cores of material from which small sharp flakes could be derived for butchery, skinning, and craftwork. Bone tools were used for sewing, tattooing, piercing, and hide processing.

When they got through the first high gap, they paused to catch their breath and beheld a vista that only the father had witnessed before. Below them lay grassy plains, braided streams, and a beaver pond bordered by red spruce and jack pine. A giant beaver, longer and heavier than any man, was repairing its dam. The man had learned from the beaver that its incisors made good woodworking tools. On the far bank a small herd of horses was grazing in a patch of sunlight. On the near bank two giant armadillos rooted among the flotsam. The misty mountain peaks and ridges beyond were bald tundra glazed and glistening with patches of snow. They looked like the blue white-capped waves he had once seen on an eastward migration to the ocean, but unmoving. *Surely the mountains and sea were related?* This was very different from the place from which they had come.

In choosing their campsite they had several important criteria—dry, flat ground, sunlight, fresh water, a wind barrier, easily foraged summer foods such as berries, roots, and aquatic fauna, and a good view of the surroundings that would allow them to defend themselves from predators such as dire wolves and large cats. They wouldn't bother hunting large game while in transit. The site they chose, on a grassy second terrace of what would later be named the South Fork of the New River, was south facing, protected from the wind by a high ridge to the west and surrounded by the bending river on the south, west, and north. A gushing icy spring issued from the rear of the terrace. On the higher ground of the terrace levee they found a place where deer had slept the previous night and knew that the deer had felt safe there. While the daughter and younger son gathered wood for the fire, the others waded

1. Paleoindian Period: 11,500–9,500 BCE

the chilly waters of an adjacent shoal to gather mussels anchored in the gravelly substrate. They also collected a large hellbender that they had inadvertently dislodged from under a rock. The mussels were shucked at the water's edge and the shells tossed into the river in order to return the spirits of the mussels to a place of rebirth. Branch-lettuce bordering the springhead provided the dinner salad.

After their repast at dusk, the four, gathered around the fire with spears at hand, joking and laughing about the mates they might find on the other side of the mountains, but occasionally interrupting their jollity to listen for the approach of a cat or wolf. They slept deeply that night, albeit with one ear turned to the night sounds.

Six days later, on their return journey, the man approached the same campsite with his sons and their new wives. As they crossed the ridge from the west, the sun was setting at their backs and a full moon was rising to welcome them. The brown tree-covered foothills below reminded him of a warm, crumbled bearskin.

The new ones spoke the same language but with a different dialect. But there was little talk as they set up camp in the waning light. While the young ones tended to the fire and food, the old man prepared his weaponry for the remaining journey. A spear tip that he had made of the black flint he had just acquired had broken when he missed his velvet-antlered quarry on a morning past. Although he was able to refashion the tip by flaking it with a deer antler tine, it was now short and ineffective, especially as a skinning and butchery knife. So, he soaked the binding sinew with his saliva, unwound it, removed the point, and placed it on the ground next to the fire. Gently, he unwrapped a new spear point from a chamois scrap in his tool bag, slotted it on the end of the spear's fore-shaft, and replaced the sinew. By morning it would be dry and fast in the haft.

******

The Paleoindian period for the larger Southeast has been variably subdivided into sub-periods, depending on a researcher's opinions about the earliest evidence of humans in the Americas. I recognize three subperiods distinguished by stone technology: Early (Pre-Clovis), Middle (Clovis and Redstone), and Late (Post-Clovis) Paleoindian. The early colonization of the Americas remains the most debated subject in American archaeology and, in part, gave rise to the discipline itself. At the time of primary European colonization, it was thought by some that Native Americans were the descendants of the ten lost tribes of Israel, exiled by King Shalmaneser in 721 BCE. In the Third Annual Report of the Bureau of Ethnology (1890), W.H. Dall suggested a first colonization by way of Polynesia (Thomas 1985). D.G. Brinton (1901:31) concluded that "at the close of the last Glacial Epoch, and for an indeterminate time previous, the comparatively shallow bed of the north Atlantic was above water; and this was about the time that we find men in the same stage of culture dwelling on both its shores." We now know, however, that dry land has not connected Europe with North America in the time of humans.

Cyrus Thomas, in his famous 1894 *Report on the Mound Explorations of the Bureau of Ethnology* (1985:727), offered this theory:

> It is therefore highly probable that a more thorough and comprehensive study of all the data bearing on the question will show, as appears to be indicated by the archaeology, that the truth lies between these opposite views; in other words, will lead to the conclusion that the continent was peopled from two sources, one part coming to the Atlantic coast, the other to the Pacific side.

The subsequent century witnessed thousands of archaeological investigations conducted by thousands of archaeologists who, with few exceptions, operated on the assumption that the Americas were first colonized by the big game-hunting "Clovis" people who migrated from northeastern Asia by way of Beringia between 12,000 and 9,000 BCE. A series of recent events and discoveries has shattered these Clovis-First and exclusively Beringian-migration paradigms. First of all, nothing similar to Clovis technology (i.e., fluted spear points such as those described below) has been found on archaeological sites in northeastern Asia. Furthermore, radiocarbon dates, artifacts, and stratigraphy at Bluefish Caves in the Yukon place humans on the continent at 24,000 BCE (Bourgeon et al. 2017). Meadowcroft Rockshelter, in western Pennsylvania (Adovasio et al. 1978), Cactus Hill, in central Virginia (McAvoy and McAvoy 2015), and several other sites in the U.S. and Mexico indisputably place humans on the American landscape by 16,000 BCE. And they had arrived in and become well adapted to southern Chile in South America by 12,800 BCE, several hundred years before Clovis, where evidence of a settlement was found at the Monte Verde site in 1975 (Dillehay 1989).

Observing similarities between stone technologies represented at Meadowcroft and Cactus Hill and those of coeval Upper Paleolithic Solutrean sites in France and Spain, Dennis Stanford, coincidentally under the same sponsorship (Smithsonian Institution) as Cyrus Thomas,

1. Paleoindian Period: 11,500–9,500 BCE

although a century later, has returned to the idea of a trans–Atlantic migration, by boat, along the edge of the glacial ice (Stanford and Bradley 2012). However, humans on both sides of the Atlantic were adapted to nearly identical Ice Age environments and would have required similar technologies to harvest resources from those environments. Until an artifact made of European flint is found in an Ice Age context in the Americas, this will remain, at best, an interesting hypothesis.

The evidence from Meadowcroft Rockshelter in western Pennsylvania clearly represents a well-established human adaptation on the edge of the Appalachian region in pre–Clovis times. Discoveries in the nearby Saltville Valley of southwestern Virginia have provided *possible* evidence of early Paleoindian (pre–Clovis) human presence dating to about 12,000 BCE. These include a fragment of a probable muskox (*Bootherium bombifrons*) tibia, which may have been used as a tool (McDonald 2000). The otherwise lack of evidence in this region may be because of: (1) little or no human use of the frigid high-elevation Appalachian Summit prior to 9,500 BCE; (2) the failure of archaeologists to recognize the evidence and distinguish it from that of later human occupation; (3) the virtual erasure of such evidence by dynamic geomorphic processes of the terminal Ice Age; or, more likely, (4) a combination of these factors. As has proven to be the case for other regions, the evidence will probably soon emerge now that more scientific minds are opening to the possibility and digging a little deeper.

Although humans had been in the Southeast as early as 18,000 years ago, the earliest evidence yet discovered in the North Carolina mountains dates to approximately 13,500 years ago. A chronology for the Paleoindian period of the Appalachian Summit is proposed as follows:

Middle Paleoindian (Clovis and Redstone): 11,500–10,800 BCE
Late Paleoindian (Hardaway and Dalton): 8,500–7,900 BCE

The oldest artifacts recovered here thus far are Clovis and Redstone spear points that date to between 11,500 and 10,800 BCE (Figure 1.2). The name "Clovis" derives from an archaeological site near Clovis, New Mexico, where similar tools were found in association with bones of wooly mammoths and other extinct Pleistocene (Ice Age) fauna. Because of this association, a potentially exaggerated picture of Paleoindian life emerged in which they were depicted as primarily "megafauna" hunters who drove the big animals to extinction. At that time a continental glacier known as the Laurentide ice sheet had expanded into Ohio and

Pennsylvania. It and other continental and alpine glaciers accounted for the loss of 300 to 400 feet of sea level. What are now the Bering Strait and the Eastern Continental Shelf were dry land (Figure 1.1). Peninsular Florida was twice its present width. Tundra extended along the crest of the Appalachians as far south as the Great Smoky Mountains (Delcourt and Delcourt 1980). The lower slopes were blanketed in a boreal forest of jack pine, spruce, and fir. A whole different suite of groceries, including horse, mastodon, peccary, giant armadillo, muskox, and caribou roamed the upland valleys and ridges. The lower elevations of the Piedmont, Valley and Ridge, and Coastal Plain sported more temperate ecosystems, even at the glacier's edge. Cyclonic winds at the glacier's edge created generally wetter conditions, cooler summers, and warmer winters for the eastern woodlands. Late Pleistocene paleontological and

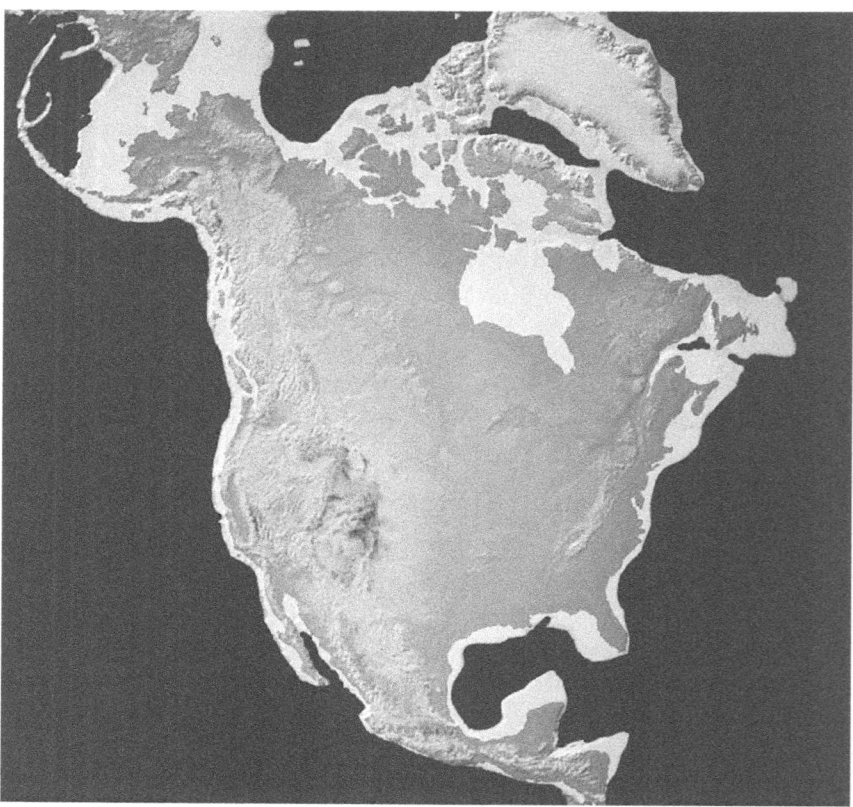

Figure 1.1. North America 18,000 years ago.

1. Paleoindian Period: 11,500–9,500 BCE

archaeological deposits on sites in or near the Appalachian highlands include remains of Pleistocene megafauna (mammoth, mastodon, giant ground sloth, horse, caribou, peccary, beautiful armadillo, etc.) and species typical of today's temperate forests (white-tailed deer, wild turkey, passenger pigeon, etc.), indicating the former existence of a complex ecological mosaic (Adovasio and Pedler 2016; Guilday et al. 1977).

Artifacts dating to the Middle and Late Paleoindian periods, including various fluted spear points and basally thinned and side-notched spear points, have been found by artifact collectors and archaeologists in the Appalachian Summit. They are found in much greater abundance, however, on the adjacent Piedmont and VRP where preferred, high quality lithic materials are more common (see Anderson and Sassaman 1996; Ledbetter et al. 1996; Perkins 1973; Turner 1989). Because they are rare, are often found on surface sites containing evidence of later human occupation, and are usually made of non-local materials (*contra* Purrington 1983) such as flint from the VRP and metavolcanic stone (dacite) from the Piedmont, citing these artifacts as evidence of Pleistocene human *presence* in the Appalachian Summit in the late Ice Age is perhaps erroneous. Evidence of scavenging, reuse, and relocation of stone tools by subsequent migratory hunter-gatherers is universally well documented, and may explain the presence of many of these items in our region (Whyte 2014; Whyte and Kimball 2017). Nevertheless, the possibility exists that artifacts were dropped in the Appalachian Summit by wide-ranging migratory Paleoindians gaining periodic access to productive quarry sites, other resources, and other humans on either side of the mountains. Sites that have yielded evidence of late Pleistocene human *occupation*, however, are situated on the fringes of the Appalachian Summit along major river valleys (Lane and Anderson 2001). These include sites in the Saltville Valley of Virginia, Dust Cave in northern

Figure 1.2. Middle Paleoindian Clovis (left) and Redstone (right) spear points.

Alabama, and the Thunderbird site in the Shenandoah Valley of Virginia. Not coincidentally, these sites are situated in proximity to high-quality lithic resources.

The last few millennia of the Pleistocene Epoch were characterized by tumultuous climate oscillations and cataclysmic geological events. Sixteen thousand years ago the Ice Age was coming to an end, or so it may have seemed. Greenland ice core data and other proxies indicate that temperatures were on a steady rise, continental glaciers were melting, sea levels were rising, and humans were steadily and unwittingly adapting to the changes. These same ice core data show a dramatic and abrupt plunge in average annual temperatures beginning at 10,800 BCE and lasting until 9,500 BCE. This climatic event, known as the Younger Dryas, was most likely initiated by an extraterrestrial impact (possibly a comet or pieces thereof). The recent discovery of a massive crater under the Greenland ice and potentially dating to the onset of the Younger Dryas may be the "smoking gun" (Kjaer et al. 2018). Wherever it occurred, this impact dislodged ice and sediment into the atmosphere and caused extensive wildfires across North America, thus preventing sunlight from warming the Earth's surface over much of the northern hemisphere. Stratified sites throughout the United States consistently reveal a layer of extraterrestrial platinum particles, nanodiamonds, and soot immediately overlying Clovis artifacts and dating to the Younger Dryas event (Moore et al. 2017). The results were generally much colder and drier winters but warmer summers in what is now temperate North America. Coincidentally, eyed bone needles used to sew leather clothing appear in the archaeological record on North American archaeological sites at approximately 10,660 BCE and disappear from the record at approximately 8,310 BCE, corresponding almost exactly with the Younger Dryas cold event (Osborn 2014). It is possible that this dramatic climatic event brought an end to Clovis culture and resulted in dramatic depopulation of humans, especially in the middle and northern latitudes of the United States. Indeed, there is very little evidence of human life in the Appalachian Summit between the start of the Younger Dryas and the beginning of the Early Archaic period—a stretch of nearly 3,000 years.

On the other side of the world, the Younger Dryas brought about a severe drought, cooler temperatures, and wild food shortages in what is now Israel and Jordan. People there had just begun to settle down in small communities and had to turn to secondary food resources (ones that require more work for less return, such as cereal grasses). Ultimately,

1. Paleoindian Period: 11,500–9,500 BCE

this led to the domestication of plants and animals that are now staple foods in our modern economies (wheat, barley, cattle, and pigs).

Artifacts of the Early Paleoindian (Pre-Clovis) Period

During times of pre–Clovis human residence in the eastern woodlands, and the same is true for any residence of any age within the region, sites would have been littered with artifacts and garbage that have long since perished (basketry, cloth, netting, bark, wood, meat, bone, antler, fur, feather, and feces). Except for a few crumbs of bone and charcoal, only stone objects have been found on most Paleoindian sites. Cautiously drawing from the evidence provided by Meadowcroft Rockshelter in western Pennsylvania (Adovasio et al. 1978) and, to a lesser extent, the Cactus Hill site in Eastern Virginia (McAvoy and McAvoy 2015), it appears that Early Paleoindian lithic technology in the eastern woodlands included medium-sized, triangular to pentagonal, un-notched spear points (Figure 1.3), flake tools, and a variety of implements derived from small, parallel-sided blades. In addition, fragments of fossil shark's teeth recovered from Cactus Hill may have been parts of tools (Whyte 1997). The projectile points recovered from Cactus Hill and the Miller point from Meadowcroft are thin and delicately pressure-flaked bifaces (tools such as knives and spear points that are flaked on both sides). The Miller point exhibits basal grinding while the Cactus Hill points are basally thinned. Both characteristics would have facilitated hafting of the points to their shafts. These points, in all respects, resemble what should be expected for the progenitors of the fluted Clovis points that would emerge in the southeastern region by 11,500 BCE.

Both Meadowcroft and Cactus Hill produced evidence of

Figure 1.3. Early Paleoindian (pre–Clovis) spear points from the Cactus Hill site, Sussex County, Virginia.

a distinctive core and blade technology. At Meadowcroft, these were made on a variety of local and nonlocal siliceous (flint-like) materials. At Cactus Hill, the expedient blades were made almost exclusively from quartzite cobbles collected from the adjacent gravel beds of the Nottoway River.

While projectile points of the Cactus Hill and Miller types have not been recognized in collections from the Appalachian Summit, it is possible that they exist but have not been distinguished from similarly-shaped later Woodland period triangular or pentagonal arrow points and knives (e.g., Greenville and Camp Creek types discussed in Chapter 5). The associated blades and blade cores, as well, are indistinguishable from those of subsequent periods. What this means is that archaeologists need to dig deeper in stratified sites in order to be able to recognize pre–Clovis components, if they exist, for what they are. Artifacts found in undisturbed stratigraphic contexts below Clovis are undeniably pre–Clovis.

Artifacts of the Middle Paleoindian Period

The large lanceolate fluted points distinctive of Middle Paleoindian culture appeared in the Appalachian Summit by approximately 11,500 BCE. It is uncertain whether fluting of projectile points originated in the Southeast or the Southwest before spreading throughout much of unglaciated North, Central, and South America. However, the vast majority has been found in the Southeast, suggesting a southeastern origin for the technology. The spear points are very carefully constructed long, thin bifaces, lanceolate to triangular in outline, and usually possess long basal thinning flake scars or "flutes" on each face (Figure 1.2). These flutes would have permitted a more streamlined haft element and prevented toggling of the point within its haft. This latter benefit indicates that the points were likely attached to fore-shafts that, when removed from the main shaft, served as butchery knives and possibly daggers.

These beautifully crafted tools are usually made of high-quality chert, jasper, chalcedony, or fine-grained dacite. Chert, jasper, and chalcedony are sedimentary rocks most locally occurring in the Knox limestone and dolomite formations of the VRP of eastern Tennessee and southwestern Virginia. Knox chert varies in color from light gray to black, is sometimes banded, and at times is nearly as lustrous

1. Paleoindian Period: 11,500–9,500 BCE

as obsidian. Because of this luster it is sometimes referred to as "flint." Red and yellow jasper, also flint-like materials, are also found among rock formations of the Piedmont Plateau, especially in Stokes County, North Carolina. Chalcedony is translucent, has a satin luster, and varies in color from white to dark gray. All of these materials are classified as cryptocrystalline rocks because individual crystals of their makeup are invisible without the aid of magnification.

The metavolcanic rocks of the Piedmont region that were used to make stone tools have been given a variety of names, such as rhyolite and vitric tuff, but and are here categorized as dacite. This material occurs in patches throughout the western and central Piedmont "Slate Belt" formations and is highly variable in color and quality (Steponaitis et al. 2006). It varies in color from greenish-gray to black, is often mottled or banded, and is relatively quick to develop a patina—a pale, chalky weathered surface.

Two types of fluted points have been found in the uplands. These include Clovis and Redstone (Figure 1.2). Clovis points typically have lanceolate shapes with slightly incurvate bases and a single flute on each side. Redstone points have more triangular shapes, more incurvate bases, and multiple overlapping flutes on each face. It is not currently known if one precedes the other chronologically. Clovis points, however, have been dated using the carbon-14 method on associated organic materials and using optically stimulated luminescence (OSL) on associated sediments. These dates range between 11,500 and 10,800 BCE.

On southeastern sites with clear evidence of Middle Paleoindian occupation, other lithic artifacts include large retouched flakes and blades, and large polyhedral cores from which these were derived (Figure 1.4). No evidence of plant processing technology such as grinding stones has been recognized for this period. Bone and ivory tools and ornaments have been recovered from anaerobic submerged sites along the southeastern coast (Dunbar and Webb 1996) and from arid caves of the interior of the continent (Driskell 1996).

Artifacts of the Late Paleoindian Period

The fluted point tradition of the Middle Paleoindian period abruptly ends during the Younger Dryas. Found above the Younger Dryas boundary on stratified sites in the Southeast are archaeological levels containing technologies similar to those of Clovis, but with notched spear points. These include Hardaway side-notched and Dalton type spear points that, like the preceding fluted points are relatively large, lanceolate or triangular in shape, and have thinned bases, but with side notches instead of flutes (Figure 1.5). Because they postdate the Younger Dryas, it might be more appropriate to assign them to the Early Archaic period or to refer to them as artifacts of a "Terminal Paleoindian" or transitional period. And, like the earlier fluted points, they are rarely found in the high elevations of the Appalachian Summit. A Hardaway Side Notched projectile point made of Piedmont dacite, along with a core-scraper of the same

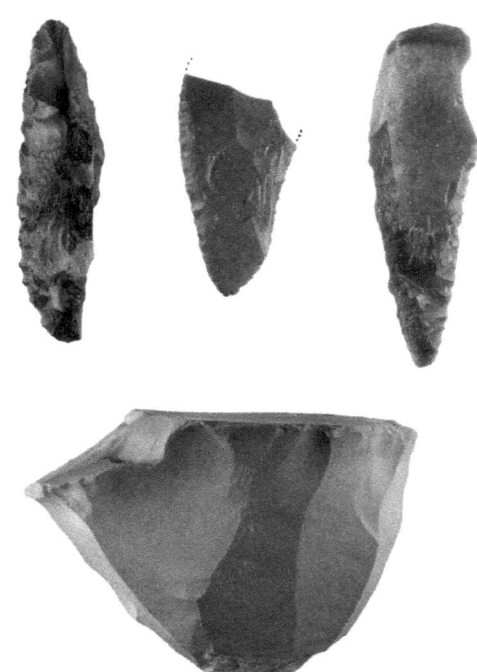

Figure 1.4. Paleoindian blade tools (top row) and a blade core (bottom).

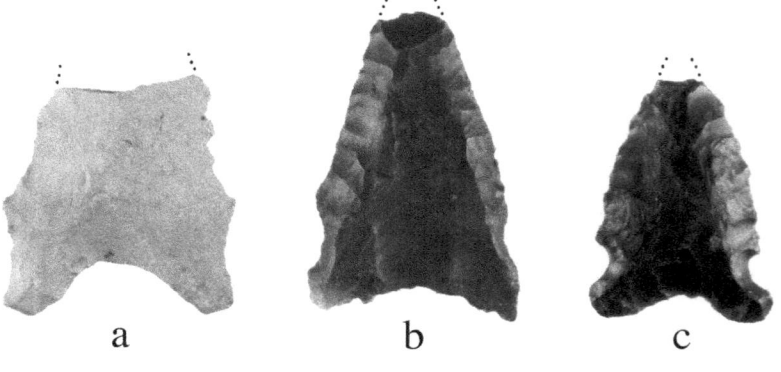

1. Paleoindian Period: 11,500–9,500 BCE

material, was found at the Gwyn Hayes site in Boone (discussed in Chapter 3). These indicate seasonal use of the uplands at the headwaters of the South Fork of the New River by hunters and gatherers migrating from the lowlands to the East. Aside from these changes in spear points, technologies of the Late Paleoindian period are nearly identical to those of the preceding.

Mountain Life in the Paleoindian Period

It is generally inferred that the earliest inhabitants of the Southeast were migratory hunter-gatherers with a broad subsistence base. Small groups of related families would have had seasonal encounters with others to exchange gifts, information, and mates. Early Paleoindian artifacts and food remains such as those from Cactus Hill and Meadowcroft provide no evidence of the "big game" subsistence focus that may have existed later and elsewhere, and which has excited the imaginations of many of the "Clovis-Firsters." Some Paleoindian sites in the southeastern lowlands have produced evidence of megafauna-hunting and use of their bones and tusks in the manufacture of tools and weaponry. Two sites near Tallahassee, Florida, have produced stone tools in association with extinct mastodon, camel, and bison bones (Halligan et al. 2016). Most of the evident food remains on Paleoindian residential sites, however, are the bones of smaller animals such as peccary, deer, turtle, and fish (e.g., Redmond and Tankersley 2005). If Clovis hunters graced the cool Appalachian Summit, it is likely that their appetites were satisfied most often by diverse fauna and flora acquired with minimum risk. The latter may have included caribou (Johnson 1996), but the rarity of fluted points in the Appalachian Mountain region, where most southeastern Pleistocene caribou remains have been identified, suggests otherwise.

Faunal remains recovered from the earliest cultural levels at Meadowcroft include bones of white-tailed deer. Bones from pre–Clovis levels at Cactus hill include those of eastern mud turtle and white-tailed deer. If the claim for evidence for pre–Clovis artifacts, features, and faunal remains from the Saltville Valley of Virginia is embraced, mastodons, muskoxen, fish, amphibians, and mollusks were on the menu (McDonald 2000).

Opposite, bottom: **Figure 1.5. Late Paleoindian Dalton (left) and Hardaway (center and right) spear points.**

Boone Before Boone

Reconstructions of Early Paleoindian settlement, based on the few known or suspected sites in the eastern uplands, are equally moot. The representation of nonlocal cherts and jaspers at Meadowcroft reflects a wide-ranging procurement (settlement) pattern similar to those that would follow in Late Paleoindian and Early Archaic times. Stone raw material needs and seasonally variable subsistence resources, as well as social interactions such as group aggregation and marriage, would have played roles in structuring the annual settlement pattern.

Prior to the Younger Dryas, Paleoindians would have had access to a variety of meat sources, including the megafauna. However, in the southeastern U.S. their tools have seldom been found in indisputable spatial association with their bones. Yet this hasn't prevented manly fantasies of nomadic big game hunters driving Pleistocene megafauna to extinction. Because of the association of highly visible fluted Points with highly discoverable mammoth remains at kill sites in the Southwest such as Clovis, New Mexico, and Naco, Arizona, archaeologists have traditionally viewed Paleoindians as having a subsistence base focused on hunting of giant Ice Age beasts. The fact that most megafauna became extinct within a couple of millennia of the "arrival" of Clovis hunters (thought by most to represent the first humans on the continent) fueled the hypothesis that humans were wholly or significantly responsible for their extinction. However, this "overkill hypothesis," spearheaded (pun intended!) by Paul S. Martin (1967), has been sufficiently discredited due to increasing evidence that the impact event of the previously discussed Younger Dryas at 10,800 BCE, just as the Ice Age was coming to a close, was the primary cause of the extinctions and brought an end to Clovis culture. Furthermore, we now know that humans were in the Americas thousands of years before the megafaunal extinctions.

Use of the Appalachian Summit region by humans in the Pleistocene may have constituted rare seasonal events of excursions between the Piedmont and VRP or exploratory forays of foragers residing in the adjacent lowlands. The region may have been included within but did not *contain* a Pleistocene human settlement system. Settlement models for the adjacent lowlands tend to agree that Paleoindian groups were characterized by wide-ranging migrations (stone tools have been found as much as 300 kilometers from quarry sources), possibly seasonally structured, and often "tethered" to geologic sources of high-quality siliceous rock (i.e., chert and jasper). More and larger sites, such as Thunderbird in the Shenandoah Valley of Virginia, are found in immediate proximity to reliable lithic sources and on the terraces of larger streams

1. Paleoindian Period: 11,500–9,500 BCE

and rivers. William Gardner (1983) uses the phrase "lithic determinism" to emphasize the importance of stone sources in structuring Paleoindian settlement. Paleoindians were "selectively mobile within a prescribed territory, with eventual return to a central base" (Gardner 1977:261). He further suggests that:

> The base camp thus becomes not only a technological resource-extraction and fabrication location, but also a center for reaffirmation and reinforcement of archaeologically identifiable group identity.... A jasper deposit, because of its fixed position, served as the point where any segment of the population could reliably predict the other segments would return to [Gardner 1977:260].

Sporadically visited hunting sites associated with Thunderbird are located in the uplands, are small and transitory in nature, and contain artifacts associated with hunting and carcass processing (Gardner 1977).

The Saltville Valley of Southwestern Virginia

If any site in or adjacent to the Appalachian Summit can claim evidence of Early Paleoindian human activity, it is SV-2 in the Saltville Valley of southwestern Virginia. Saltville is located in the VRP and is underlain and flanked primarily by carbonate limestone, ideal geology for preservation of organic remains. The valley is well known for its late Pleistocene paleontological deposits and its relative abundance of Middle Paleoindian fluted projectile points. Site SV-2, situated at an elevation of 1,720 feet and located adjacent to the channel of the former Saltville River, was excavated by the Virginia Museum of Natural History from 1992 to 1997 (McDonald 2000). Three horizons potentially containing evidence of Early Paleoindian activity have been radiocarbon dated to between 12,510 and 11,000 BCE. The evidence includes flakes and possible tools of exogenous (non-local) chert, possible bone tools, and an unusual concretion of bone and sediment. One fragment of probably a muskox (*Bootherium bombifrons*) tibia is spirally fractured and exhibits, along its sharp fractured edge, polish and striations resulting from "extensive abrasive contact with soft animal tissue" (McDonald 2000:45). This specimen was radiocarbon dated to 14,510 ± 80 years before present (approximately 12,500 BCE). Unfortunately, spirally fractured, polished, and striated bone fragments are known to result from natural processes, including consumption and digestion by large carnivores, and locomotion following traumatic injury. One alone does not constitute evidence of human use. Another aspect of the site that calls into question its validity is its complex and interrupted stratigraphy; the associations of dated materials with possible anthropogenic objects and deposits is tenuous. If humans were in the Saltville Valley prior to 13,000 years ago, there must be better evidence.

In the event that SV-2 is validated by discovery of additional sites in the valley, then humans were likely making regular visits to enjoy the natural salt deposits and, more likely, large herbivores attracted to salt. Sources of high-quality Knox chert, occurring in and around the Saltville Valley, also may have attracted pre–Clovis hunters. Artifacts of this material are abundant on nearly every precontact archaeological site in the area.

The Colvard II Site, Ashe County, North Carolina

The slightest indication of Paleoindian visitation to the Appalachian Summit was found at the Colvard II site along the South Fork of the New River in Ashe County, North Carolina (Whyte 2010a). Permission to explore the site was generously given by Annabel Harrill, whose father, Fred Colvard, had collected many artifacts from it and other sites in the vicinity. Although the site had been plowed, when it was explored by ASU archaeologists it was covered in tall grass, necessitating systematic interval testing with small test pits spaced on even intervals. Screening of the soil from the test pits revealed two concentrations of stone artifacts and pottery. These two areas were gridded in 1 × 1 m squares and excavated to the base of the plow zone. Although many artifacts representing many time periods were found, at the very base of the plow zone in one part of the site, three particularly early stone artifacts were recovered—two large scrapers and a drill—that are of types typically found with fluted points in the region (Figure 1.6). Another indication of their early age is that they are made of materials derived from very far away. One large scraper was made from a blade of Newman chert that originated in eastern Kentucky, over 200 kilometers from the site. Another large scraper was made on a blade of dacite from the Carolina Piedmont near Asheboro, North Carolina, approximately 160 kilometers from the site. This indicates that the hunters and gatherers who visited the site migrated over very large distances to obtain their needs, one of which was high-quality lithic material. Although no fluted points were found at Colvard II, they have

1. Paleoindian Period: 11,500–9,500 BCE

Figure 1.6. Paleoindian blade tools and drill (center) from the Colvard 2 site, Ashe County, North Carolina.

been found by collectors on other sites in the surrounding New River valley.

The Birckhead Site, Watauga County, North Carolina

Along the South Fork of the New River, just outside of Boone, North Carolina, an artifact collector found a Clovis point of Knox black chert on the surface of a plowed field (Figure 1.7). This is one of few fluted points reported for the county, and the only one for which a general provenience of discovery is documented. The artifact may have been deposited by its maker in the late Ice Age. Alternatively, it was found elsewhere and at a later time in prehistory, reused, and redeposited at the Birckhead site.

Artifact collectors often wonder why a seemingly perfect (unbroken) projectile point would have been discarded. Realize, however, that the Birckhead Clovis point, when first made, may have been two to three times as long. During its use, as it became dull or damaged, it may have been sharpened many times by flaking the blade edges, thus reducing it to its final discarded form.

Recently ASU archaeologists returned to the Birckhead site to determine if other evidence from the Paleoindian period could be found. At that time the broad floodplain on which the Clovis point had been found was covered in tall grass and weeds, so the archaeologists decided to excavate small test pits through the plow zone at ten-meter intervals across the site. In screening the soil, they recovered projectile points and other artifacts indicating evidence of a slightly later (Early Archaic period) encampment. Ironically, they recovered an Early Archaic Kirk Corner Notched spear point that had been recycled from a scavenged fluted Clovis point of Piedmont dacite (Figure 1.8) (Whyte and Kimball 2017). This suggests the possibility that the Clovis point found on the same site had been scavenged and relocated but not refashioned into a new type of spear point.

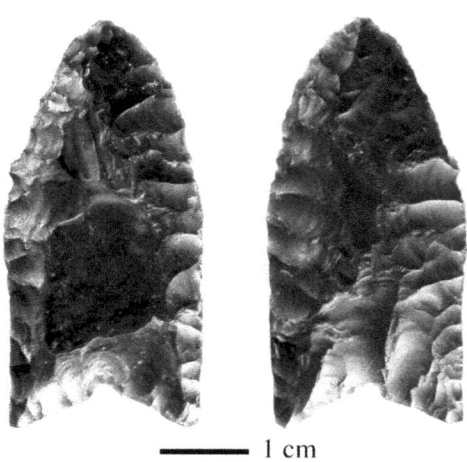

── 1 cm

Figure 1.7. The Birckhead Clovis point.

── 1 cm

Figure 1.8. Early Archaic Kirk spear point recycled from a fluted point.

The Thunderbird Site, Shenandoah Valley, Virginia

In the early 1970s archaeologists from the Catholic University of America and Thunderbird Research Associates, Inc. conducted

1. Paleoindian Period: 11,500–9,500 BCE

archaeological investigations at the Flint Run Paleoindian Complex near Front Royal, in the Shenandoah Valley of Virginia (Gardner 1977). Thunderbird, the primary base camp and quarry site of the complex, is situated on a terrace of the South Fork of the Shenandoah River, a few kilometers upstream of its confluence with the North Fork. The site was occupied periodically between about 9,200 and 7,500 BCE primarily for the purpose of quarrying Flint Run jasper and working it into finished tools and weaponry. Among the earliest artifacts recovered from the site are numerous Clovis points and point fragments. Some were broken or exhausted in use and repeated sharpening, while others were broken in manufacture. Paleoindians were undoubtedly attracted to Flint Run jasper for its accessibility, tractability and beautiful yellow color. Moreover, the source is located in proximity to rich ecotones of the Blue Ridge and the expansive river valley, which must have guaranteed availability of food and other necessities.

Lanceolate, fluted spear points from Thunderbird have concave and slightly flared bases and, like fluted points from throughout North America, are heavily ground or smoothed along the hafting margin. This prevented tearing of hafting sinews and splitting of the shaft on impact. Experimental replication studies reveal that fluting of the base was achieved by percussion with a "soft hammer" such as an antler baton or "billet" (Johnson 1996).

The artifact assemblage from Thunderbird consists entirely of lithic items resulting from quarrying and retooling. No food remains such as bone or plant material survived the ravages of time and climate on this open-air site. Notwithstanding, Gardner (1977:261) is able to place the site within a settlement and subsistence context:

> The Flint Run Complex settlement system does not support the view of Paleoindians as highly mobile big-game hunters, constantly in pursuit of game. These populations were mobile, to be sure, but they were selectively mobile within a prescribed territory, with eventual return to a central base. The wandering was not specifically seasonally oriented as we can ascribe to Middle Archaic and later populations, but it was to some degree scheduled with the scheduling tied into tool-kit depletion, social needs, and other factors.

Summary

Off the northeast coast of Siberia in the Chukchi Sea is the Island of Kotelny. During the late Ice Age, when global sea levels were nearly

Boone Before Boone

400 feet lower, this island was a promontory just west of the Bering Strait land bridge or "Beringia." Approximately 20,000 years ago hunters killed and butchered a mammoth there (*Siberian Times* 2019). On the American side of Beringia is a site in Yukon called "Bluefish Caves," where archaeologists discovered stone tools and butchered mammoth bones dating to 24,000 years ago (Bourgeon et al. 2017). Together, this evidence indicates that *Homo sapiens* hunter-gatherers in what is now Siberia gradually expanded in to the Americas by way of Beringia sometime prior to 24,000 years ago. The skeletal remains of a human child found near Lake Baikal in southern Siberia, also dating to 24,000 years ago, contained preserved DNA segments that were sequenced and shown to be related to today's Native Americans (*Siberian Times* 2013). Together, this evidence indicates that *Homo sapiens* hunter-gatherers in what is now Siberia gradually expanded in to the Americas by way of Beringia sometime prior to 24,000 years ago. Some spread through the interior, as suggested by the evidence form Bluefish Caves, while others spread along the coastline as indicated by human footprints on Calvert Island, British Columbia, dating to 13,000 years ago (McLaren et al. 2018).

Humans resided in the lower elevations and gentler climes of the Eastern United States as early as 17,000 BCE, during the maximum advance of Ice Age glaciation. Human occupation of or visitation to the Appalachian Summit in the late Pleistocene Epoch is barely in evidence. The few dozen Clovis, Dalton, and Hardaway projectile points recovered are, for the most part, isolated finds which may have been scavenged and brought in from elsewhere by later Archaic period visitors to the uplands. Most of these points are made of Knox formation chert, Shady formation jasper, or Piedmont dacite, which naturally occur in immediately adjacent regions but *not* within the Appalachian Summit as defined. The region was perhaps sporadically transited or explored by very small groups of hunters going beyond the reaches of their traditional territorial range, which may have brushed the ecologically rich and variable lower foothills of the Appalachian Summit margin. The paucity of evidence of these early Native Americans may, in part, be due to dramatic weathering events of the late Ice Age that resulted in mudslides, debris flows, and flood scouring that would have deeply buried or washed away the sites and their contents.

By 9,500 BCE the Younger Dryas and the Pleistocene Epoch came to an end, continental and alpine glaciers began to melt, temperatures and sea levels began to rise, and the Appalachian Summit slowly began

1. Paleoindian Period: 11,500–9,500 BCE

to change from a boreal, coniferous forest and tundra environment to one dominated by oak, hickory, chestnut, and beech trees. And the few remaining Pleistocene beasts of the region that had survived the Younger Dryas impact, one by one, became extinct.

2

Early Archaic Period: 8,000–6,000 BCE

The small group arrived at the new camp in late afternoon, smelling much like the oak leaves that were beginning to litter the ground around them. Their tanned skins and leather garments, like their oaken smell, provided camouflage as they moved through the shadowy autumn forest. Their wagging blue-black braids tied with braided milkweed twine, like horse's tails kept the flies from gaining purchase. No one spoke as the two families, including seven adults and five children, set about unloading their gear, clearing the space, and gathering fallen limbs and twigs for the fire. Their two pack dogs, relieved of their burdens, eagerly drank from the adjacent spring.

They were hunters and gatherers who migrated with the seasonal changes. When the beeches, chestnuts, and maples began to splash the forests in the uplands with red and gold, the group would come to this campsite, year after year, to spend ten to twenty days hunting deer, turkey, and squirrels and gathering chestnuts and herbs for immediate use and to dry meats and make nut cakes for later consumption. They had no leader, although the older men and women were responsible for decisions that affected the group as a whole—when to relocate, where to hunt, and negotiations with other small groups they would encounter in their migrations.

They came to this place again because it had served them well in previous years; it had a name and it was along their well-trodden path, there was fresh water and a clearing in the trees that provided warm sunlight, and there was an abundance of chestnut trees whose nuts attracted squirrels, turkeys, raccoons, and deer. There also were two small rock shelters nearby that would provide refuge should a storm threaten. And since they had stayed here many times before, there were many useful things on the ground, such as grinding cobbles, hammer stones, anvil stones, and pieces of chert that could be used again. Some

2. Early Archaic Period: 8,000–6,000 BCE

of the artifacts that lay at their feet and that they would re-use were over five hundred years old.

When they had settled, a woman unwrapped her fire-starting kit from a scrap of deer hide. It contained a basswood palette, a cane spindle, and a wad of tinder consisting of shredded cedar bark. She picked up a sharp chert flake from the ground—one that had been used for various purposes on previous visits to the site—and cut a small notch in the palette. She then squatted with her calloused feet on either end of the palette, spat on the palms of her calloused, fissured hands, and began to rigorously spin the cane spindle with its tip in the notch. In half a minute a wisp of blue smoke wafted up from the blackening notch and a small ember was spilled into the wad of cedar bark. Gently, she cupped the wad in her hands and blew the ember into a blaze. This was then placed in the same hearth that had been used on many visits prior. Dry leaves, small twigs, and then branches were added to fuel the fire that would warm and feed them for many days. At night, four other fires would be ignited from this one to keep the people warm as they slept on the ground close by.

Meanwhile, the children upturned rocks in the creek and caught several large crayfish that would become part of the evening's repast. The group would also eat dried venison and nut cakes that they had brought to the site, as well as two box turtles and several mushrooms that they had encountered along the path.

While women tended the fires and prepared the food, the four men in the group began to gear up for tomorrow's hunt. This involved sharpening spear tips and knives and making replacements for broken or exhausted tools. Most of their tools were in good order; they had prepared well before leaving the big valley to the west where black chert, yellow and red jasper, and translucent chalcedony were in abundance. Here in the mountains, only quartz could be chipped into sharp tools such as spear points. To find good pieces of quartz that had no cracks, they would search the gravel bars along the river for white cobbles and pebbles that had been tumbled and smoothed by the rapids, for these had survived the battering of rock against rock for ages. Their tools would have to sustain them until they migrated further east, onto the Piedmont Plateau, where an abundance of dacite would serve to replenish their tool supply.

In the morning, after the men left camp for the deer hunt, the women and children would find what they needed to build three small huts, like inverted bark-covered baskets of woven branches. The rotted remains of last year's structures that lay in heaps on the ground would have to be cleared away.

In the following days they would kill several deer, turkeys and squirrels. The men would hunt deer with their spears and spear throwers. Women would forage the forest floor for nuts, herbs, roots, and turtles. Children would hunt squirrels with their blowguns. Turkeys would be snatched from their roosting branches at night. Squirrel and turkey meat and deer organs and bone marrow would be eaten during their residence at the camp. Deer meat would be dried in strips over the fires to preserve it for consumption while in transit and at their winter residence off the mountain to the east. Deer sinews, hides, antlers, and some bones would provide raw materials for tools and clothing. This was a way of life that would last for another eight thousand years in the Appalachian Summit.

******

Ten thousand years ago the Appalachian Summit region had become a very rich and tolerable place for human life. Continental glaciers had retreated and northern hardwood forests and their associated biota gradually replaced the boreal environment. The megafauna, excepting humans, had become extinct or extirpated from the region. The climate was seasonally more variable with much warmer summers, slightly cooler winters, and less annual rainfall.

The early Holocene climatic Epoch correlates with the Early Archaic period (8,000–6,000 BCE) as defined by archaeology. The term *Archaic* was first proffered by New York archaeologist William Ritchie (1932) to describe human time in the eastern woodlands after the Ice Age but before the widespread use of ceramic technology. Its beginning and end vary regionally and among researchers. William Gardner (1989), for example, considers the Early Archaic period (as represented at the Flint Run Paleoindian Complex in Virginia) as a continuation of the Paleoindian period, preferring to call it a sub-period of the Paleoindian period.

The Appalachian Summit Early Archaic period consists of at least four, temporally distinct phases marked by distinctive spear point types: Lower Kirk Corner Notched, Upper Kirk Corner Notched (Figure 2.1), St. Albans, and LeCroy (Figure 2.2). The latter two represent the Bifurcate Point Tradition as defined by discoveries at the deeply stratified St. Albans site in West Virginia (Broyles 1971). Considering data from stratified sites of the Tellico Reservoir Project in eastern Tennessee (Kimball 1985) and the St. Albans site just west of Charleston, West Virginia

2. Early Archaic Period: 8,000–6,000 BCE

Figure 2.1. Early Archaic Lower Kirk (left) and Upper Kirk (right) spear points.

Figure 2.2. Early Archaic St. Albans (left) and LeCroy (right) spear points.

(Broyles 1971), and based primarily on spear point type changes, a chronology for the Early Archaic period of the Appalachian Summit is proposed as follows:

Lower Kirk: 8,000–7,000 BCE
Upper Kirk: 7,500–7,000 BCE
St. Albans: 7,000–6,500 BCE
LeCroy: 6,500–6,000 BCE

Other Early Archaic spear point types defined in contiguous regions, such as the Palmer type described by Coe (1964) for the Piedmont Plateau in central North Carolina and the MacCorkle bifurcate described by Broyles (1971) for the Cumberland Plateau to the west are found in minor numbers in the Appalachian Summit. To the south of the Appalachian Summit, Dust Cave in northern Alabama produced evidence of a very Early Archaic component (8,000 BCE) characterized by side-notched spear points (Driskell 1996). This was stratigraphically overlain by a Kirk Corner Notched component (Sherwood et al. 2004). These points are very similar to Kessell Side-Notched points, which also precede corner notched points in West Virginia (Broyles 1966).

Lower Kirk Phase

Kirk Corner Notched projectile points were named for the Kirk family colonial homestead located near the Hardaway site in Stanly County, North Carolina (Coe 1964). Defined by contexts and artifacts at the Icehouse Bottom and Bacon Farm sites in Loudoun County, Tennessee (Chapman 1977), the Lower Kirk phase is characterized by corner notched spear points with excurvate, heavily ground bases and (often) recurvate serrated blades (Figure 2.1). These spear points occur stratigraphically below Upper Kirk points. Lower Kirk points found in the Appalachian Summit are often made on chert and jasper derived from the VRP. Examples made of locally abundant vein quartz also are common. This phase has been dated to between 8,000 and 7,000 BCE. Other stone tools commonly found with these projectile points are long blades of chert with cutting and scraping edges, end scrapers that would have been hafted for hide processing (Figure 2.3), and hammers, anvils, and

Figure 2.3. Early Archaic end scrapers.

seed grinding stones. Less common are small ground stone celts (axe blades) and adze blades used in woodworking.

Upper Kirk Phase

Projectile points of the Upper Kirk strata at Icehouse Bottom and Bacon Farm include two very similar forms: a small haft variety and a slightly later large haft variety (Chapman 1977; Kimball 1996). These have straight or concave bases, which may or may not be edge-ground (Figure 2.1). The associated lithic tool kit is very similar to that of Lower Kirk. Likewise, Upper Kirk points found in the Appalachian Summit are often made on VRP chert and jasper, Piedmont rhyolite, and vein quartz. This phase has been dated to between 7,500 and 7,000 BCE.

St. Albans Phase

The St. Albans phase marks the beginning of a tradition of making basally-notched "bifurcate" projectile points. Named for the type-site on the Cumberland Plateau of West Virginia (Broyles 1971), St. Albans points are corner notched and basally-notched, with basal lobes angling down and out from the vertical axis (Figure 2.2). The lobes and notches are usually edge-ground. Blades are usually serrated and often asymmetrically sharpened. Specimens found in the Appalachian Summit are often made of vein quartz or VRP chert. This phase has been dated to between 7,000 and 6,500 BCE.

This and the subsequent phases of the Early Archaic period are also characterized by frequent evidence of bipolar (hammer-and-anvil) reduction of lithic raw materials to produce sharp, sometimes prismatic flakes, and wedges used in the splitting of bone, antler, and wood. This was achieved by holding a nodule of chert or other material on a flat anvil stone and striking the top with a hammer.

LeCroy Phase

The LeCroy phase is a continuation of the bifurcate point tradition. LeCroy points are very similar to their precursors. The bases are deeply notched and the basal lobes curve inward terminally, often forming a point at the basal notch (Figure 2.2). Basal grinding is infrequent. The hafting element (below the blade) on these points is remarkably consistent in size and shape from New England to Georgia, suggesting the possibility that they were hafted to fore-shafts that were made of something of consistent size such as a deer metatarsus (a long bone of the hind foot) or turkey tibiotarsus (a long bone of the leg). This phase has been dated to between 6,500 and 6,000 BCE.

Artifacts of the Early Archaic Period

The projectile points of the Early Archaic are similar to the fluted points that preceded them only in the quality of manufacture and the continued preference for cryptocrystalline silica material. The notable difference is a complete switch to notching of the base and frequent serration of the blade. Gardner has proposed that the practice of notching signifies the switch from the thrusting spear or javelin to the spear thrower or, to use the Aztec word, "atlatl." An atlatl is a stick, sometimes weighted, with a hook at the distal end. With the hook inserted into the hollowed shaft of a spear or dart, the atlatl provided extra leverage and thrust in the propulsion of the spear (Figure 2.4). Atlatls were used by hunters and warriors around the world and, in Australia, well into the twentieth century. Only extensive experimentation and studies of impact traces and breakage will determine if Gardner is correct. Frequent serration and asymmetrical sharpening of the blade edges, however, indicate that these points also functioned as knives. Notching protected the binding of the stone point by isolating it from the heavily used cutting edge of the tool. It also served to extend the length of the cutting edge. An Early Archaic, notched projectile point hafted in a foreshaft could have been readily detached from the spear shaft and used as a hafted knife in processing the fresh kill, thus reducing the required tool kit to a single, portable composite—an important advantage to highly mobile hunter-gatherers (Figure 2.5). The basal notch of the bifurcate points would have conferred additional stability in resisting the lateral pressure imposed by cutting. Pressure applied to the edge would have been countered by pressure of the basal lobe toggling against the shaft. Micro-traces of projection and butchery were observed on Early Archaic points from the Main site on the Cumberland Plateau of southeastern Kentucky (Kimball 1994). This further indicates the duel functions of these tools.

2. Early Archaic Period: 8,000–6,000 BCE

Figure 2.4. Atlatl (spear thrower) replica in use.

Aside from the variably notched projectile point forms discussed above, Early Archaic stone tool kits in the Appalachian Summit included bifacially flaked knives and drills, hide scrapers, assorted blade and flake tools (Figure 2.6), ground minerals such as hematite and graphite used for red paint pigment (Figure 2.7), ground stone celts, and a variety of cobble tools (Figure 2.8). Products and byproducts of bipolar flaking (wedges, flakes, cores, and pitted cobbles) are also conspicuous on Early Archaic base camps, increasing in evidence while blade technology decreases throughout the period (Kimball 1996). Chipped stone artifacts, like those of the preceding Paleoindian period, are more often made on cryptocrystalline materials (chert, chalcedony, and jasper) obtained from adjacent regions.

The first concrete evidence of ceramic and fiber technologies in the region is found on Early Archaic sites such as Icehouse Bottom in Tennessee and Dust Cave in Alabama (Sherwood and Chapman 2005). At each of these base-camp sites, prepared clay surfaces were identified, some retaining textile impressions made before firing (Figure 2.9). These flattened lenses of fired clay may have been constructed by flattening clay on a mat or other fabric surface, inverting it, and then heating it to 500°C or more. Another possibility is that the clay was spread out on the ground and then a fabric was pressed into its surface to give it a texture

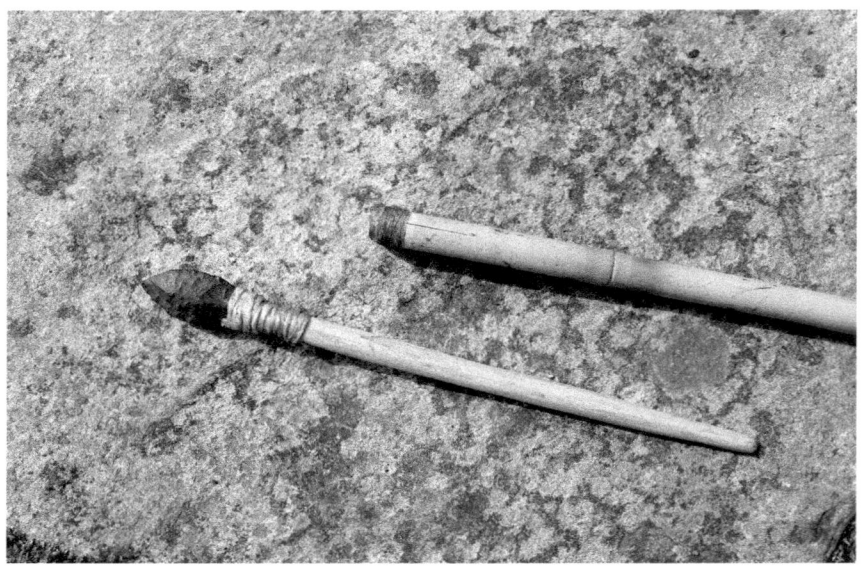

Figure 2.5. Removal of the fore-shaft from an atlatl dart.

or perhaps for symbolism. The resulting hardened clay surface may have functioned as a relatively clean cooking surface that could be reheated with embers, much like the late precontact griddles (Palometta Ware) of the Bahamas (Winter 1978). Textile impressions preserved at Dust Cave, northern Alabama, include a possible split cane warp with two-twist fiber wefts.

Figure 2.6. Early Archaic drills (top row) and end scrapers (bottom row).

2. Early Archaic Period: 8,000–6,000 BCE

Those from Icehouse Bottom include a fiber net-like simple twining with two-twist wefts (Figure 2.9). These objects are found in the Kirk phase components at Icehouse Bottom and in all Early and Middle Archaic strata at Dust Cave (Sherwood and Chapman 2005). None has yet been identified in association with the Bifurcate tradition.

Experiments undertaken to determine the possible function of these objects were undertaken by Homsey et al. (2010) and ASU's Experimental Archaeology students (unpublished). The experimental surfaces proved ineffective in cooking meats unless the meats were covered in hot coals (Homsey and Sherwood 2010; Homsey et al. 2010). The heated experimental surfaces did, however, prove effective in baking acorn and chestnut cakes, which were known to have been an important storable and portable fall-season food for many Native American groups. It is likely that Early and

Figure 2.7. Ground hematite and graphite nodules from the Dutch Creek site, Watauga County, North Carolina.

Figure 2.8. Hammer (top row) and anvil (bottom row) stones from the Dutch Creek site, Watauga County, North Carolina.

Figure 2.9. Early Archaic textile-impressed fired clay slab from the Icehouse Bottom site, Loudoun County, Tennessee (courtesy of the Frank H. McClung Museum of Natural History & Culture, University of Tennessee, Knoxville).

Middle Archaic groups harvesting nuts in the Appalachian Summit highlands in the fall employed similar technology. However, no buried Early Archaic base camps at which such evidence would potentially be preserved have yet been discovered in these higher elevations.

Tools and utensils of antler, bone, and wood were undoubtedly part of the Early Archaic equipment but have not been found preserved in the Appalachian Summit region. Considering the evidence from Dust Cave, however, Appalachian Summit residents likely made use of awls and projectile points constructed from large bird and mammal long bones (Goldman-Finn and Walker 1994). The cane and net impressions found in the fired clay are the earliest evidence of cane and fiber working in the region; however, it is assumed that basketry, mats, and nets of much variety were part of the Early Archaic period cultural repertoire.

Mountain Life in the Early Archaic Period

Unlike the preceding Paleoindian period, there is clear and abundant evidence of human presence in the Appalachian Summit in the

2. Early Archaic Period: 8,000–6,000 BCE

Early Holocene. Sites are found on all major landform categories, in rockshelters, and in the open. Possibly because of erosion, burial, and the failure of archaeologists to invest in deep site explorations, no Early Archaic base-camp sites, probably situated on terraces of larger rivers, have been located in the Appalachian Summit. They do occur in riverine and upland settings of the adjacent VRP and Cumberland Plateau regions in proximity to resource-rich ecotones. Unfortunately, the nature and degree of the presence of Early Archaic peoples in the Appalachian Summit are obscured by typological confusion; some Late Archaic Brewerton phase projectile points, also abundant in the region, are similarly notched with heavily ground bases, but are more often made of quartz, quartzite, or rhyolite (Chapter 4). The failure of researchers to distinguish later Brewerton from earlier Kirk points in the southern Appalachians has resulted in an erroneous inflation of estimates of Early Archaic site numbers and population densities, and a misinterpretation of Early Archaic settlement and subsistence in the region. The position that the Appalachian Summit supported a resident population beginning with the Kirk phase (Purrington 1983), for example, may be a product of this typological mixing.

Reliable data provided by Bass (1977) and Kimball (1996) indicate *seasonal* use of the Appalachian summit by migratory hunter-gatherers (Figure 2.10). The frequent recovery of Early Archaic points made of VRP cryptocrystalline lithic materials and Piedmont dacite in the region indicates migration territories overlapping adjacent physiographic provinces. Indeed, Anderson and Hanson (1988) see the mountains as a territorial frontier in the Early Archaic. As Gardner (1977) suggested for the Paleoindian and Early Archaic periods (as manifested at the Flint Run site complex in Virginia's Shenandoah Valley), larger residential base camps may have been situated in proximity to reliable lithic sources, while smaller, more temporary foraging and hunting camps were often located in the uplands.

Early Archaic sites found in the higher elevations of the Appalachian Summit probably represent warm season (spring through fall) foraging bases, hunting stands, and kill/processing sites; many are found in gaps where mountain passes facilitated the movement of game and humans. Winter-season base camps, almost of necessity, would have been situated below the Appalachian Summit elevations.

Kimball (1996), in reference to the Tellico Reservoir project in the VRP of eastern Tennessee, notes evidence of a shift in site distributions between Kirk and Bifurcate times in the Early Archaic. The earlier Kirk

Figure 2.10. Artist's reconstruction of an Early Archaic campsite (courtesy of the Frank H. McClung Museum of Natural History & Culture, University of Tennessee, Knoxville; drawing by Tom Whyte).

phase sites are widely distributed across different landforms whereas bifurcate phase sites may be more common along secondary tributaries in the uplands. Thus, he warns, we should not generalize about an Early Archaic settlement pattern for the region.

Early Archaic subsistence remains are uncommon in the Southeast and all but lacking in evidence in the Appalachian Summit. This dearth is mostly attributable to poor preservation in acidic, moist environments. Thus, it is again necessary to draw conclusions from evidence in adjacent regions graced with better preservation. The basic soils and protective karst of the adjacent VRP and Cumberland Plateau regions are particularly generous in this regard. Evidence from Dust Cave in northern Alabama, numerous rockshelters in eastern Kentucky, and buried floodplain sites provide evidence of a broad-based forager economy.

Carbonized nutshells of acorn, hickory, walnut, butternut, and chestnut are relatively abundant on Early Archaic base-camp sites

2. Early Archaic Period: 8,000–6,000 BCE

in adjacent regions. Nuts gathered in the late summer may have been stored or processed into meal for later fall or winter consumption. An abundance of nutshells on these sites indicates that some base camps were occupied at least in late summer. The prepared clay surfaces found at Icehouse Bottom and Dust Cave may have been used to cook flat breads and cakes made, in part, from nut meal. Flat river cobbles with depressed surfaces, found on many of the larger sites, probably functioned as seed and nut grinding stones or "metátes." Wild pigweed and knotweed seeds may have been ground to make flour. Seeds of fruits such as wild grape and pokeweed also have been found in Early Archaic components (Chapman and Shea 1981).

Animal remains found on Early Archaic sites in the broader region represent the entire gamut of vertebrates and invertebrates. Unfortunately, most of this evidence comes from cave and rockshelter sites where nonhuman mammalian denizens may have contributed their skeletal remains and those of their prey. Considering that the modern Holocene faunal suite had essentially emplaced itself, Early Archaic visitors to the Appalachian summit undoubtedly structured their subsistence and settlement systems, in part, around white-tailed deer. Deer not only would have provided the most protein, but also hide, antler, bone, and sinew.

Early Archaic human burials found near the Appalachian Summit include two cremations, one associated with Upper Kirk and one associated with LeCroy, at the Icehouse Bottom site (Chapman 1977). These were found in shallow graves and each appears to represent an adult female. One also contained cremated animal bone. It is possible that other shallow pits excavated nearby but which contained no bones were the graves of in-flesh burials; cremated or "calcined" bone is often all that remains preserved from early deposits (Whyte 2001). The individuals represented by the two cremations may have died and were cremated far afield to facilitate their transportation to and ultimate interment at a culturally prescribed location such as the base camp. Alternatively, cremation followed by burial on-site may have been the preferred mortuary treatment in the Early Archaic period.

The Dutch Creek Site and Church Rockshelter No. 1, Watauga County, North Carolina

The fictional narrative that introduces this chapter is based on evidence from the Dutch Creek site (Figure 2.11) overlooking the

Boone Before Boone

confluence of Dutch Creek with Watauga River near Valle Crucis, North Carolina (Whyte 2013a). Church Rockshelter No. 1 (Figure 2.12) opens up toward Watauga River on a hillside nearby (Whyte 2013b). Archaeologists found evidence of Early Archaic period occupation at both sites. The Dutch Creek site contains evidence of seasonal use throughout the Holocene Epoch. The view that it commands of the confluence of Dutch Creek with Watauga River and the expansive floodplains to the northwest and southeast was clearly a primary reason for its frequent use. The movements of prey and human travelers could be monitored from this elevated vantage even if it was forested. Indeed, the stone artifacts recovered, while representing only the inorganic component of what had been deposited by ancient humans, are the classic suite characteristic of an upland seasonal camp.

In the Early Archaic period the site was used by small groups of hunter-gatherers whose cycle of migration included the VRP 30 kilometers downriver and to the west where they could obtain high quality chert, jasper, and chalcedony for their toolkits. Stone artifacts found at the site, all from within twenty centimeters of the surface,

Figure 2.11. Westward view of the Dutch Creek site, Watauga County, North Carolina.

2. Early Archaic Period: 8,000–6,000 BCE

Figure 2.12. Church Rockshelter No. 1, Watauga County, North Carolina.

include hundreds of flakes of chert, chalcedony, and jasper. These include bifacial thinning flakes detached in the making and resharpening of tools such as spear points and knives, flakes detached from cores to be used as expedient tools, and bipolar flakes resulting from tool recycling and economizing—getting the most usable material out of precious resources. In addition, hammer and anvil stones used in the bipolar reduction process were found (Figure 2.8). Chipped stone tools recovered include the bases of two Lower Kirk Corner Notched spearpoints (Figure 2.13 a & b), a unifacially retouched blade (c), and an end scraper (d). A ground pebble of graphite and one of hematite indicate the processing of black and red pigments, possibly mixed with oils for body paint (Figure 2.7). Burnt river cobbles found scattered throughout the site were once clustered as hearths used for cooking and warmth.

The two Kirk Corner Notched projectile points recovered are made of Knox formation chert. One is nearly complete and exhibits a patch of residual cortex on one face, indicating that it was made from a flake or thin nodule derived from a bedrock source. The specimen exhibits an extensively reworked and serrated blade and a lightly ground excurvate base. The other specimen includes only the basal portion, is burnt, and also exhibits a lightly ground excurvate base. Because of the basal excurvation, these are more specifically assignable to the "Lower Kirk" type defined by Chapman (1977) and dating to approximately 7,500 BCE.

Two other chipped stone tools likely associated with this Lower Kirk component are an end-scraper (Figure 2.13 d) and a triangular unifacially retouched blade that appears to have been used in woodworking (Figure 2.13 c), each made of VRP chert (probably from the Knox Group Dolomite) that may have come from eastern Tennessee or southeastern Kentucky. The end-scraper was made from a decortication flake of a mottled, fossiliferous, grayish brown chert that does not resemble the typical black, gray, and banded varieties documented for the Knox dolomites. The triangular blade tool is made of a dark grayish brown banded chert that resembles samples collected from the northern end of Norris Reservoir in Campbell County, Tennessee, over 200 kilometers to the west. Such blade tools made of exogenous chert are usually found only on late Pleistocene and Early Holocene sites in the region (Whyte 2010a).

Additional artifacts likely dating to the Early Archaic period are the six pitted cobbles (anvils) and abundant compression flakes recovered. These appear to be the results of bipolar percussion, primarily of chert, and are most often the products of Early Archaic period lithic industries in the southern Appalachian region (Chapman 1975). At the Dutch Creek site, bipolar percussion was probably undertaken to maximize the material provision of highly coveted exogenous cherts.

2. Early Archaic Period: 8,000–6,000 BCE

Figure 2.13. Early Archaic chipped-stone tools from the Dutch Creek site, Watauga County, North Carolina.

Recovery of similar artifacts in the deepest strata of Church Rockshelter No. 1, situated only 70 meters to the east, indicates that the two sites may have been visited by the same or closely related people. There, several Kirk Corner Notched points of chert, jasper, chalcedony, and quartz were recovered (Figure 2.14), along with pitted cobbles used in the bipolar flaking technique, cobbles used as grinding stones, and various chipped stone tools.

Summary

Projectile point types that define the local Early Archaic period are found throughout the eastern United States, suggesting a shared concept of what these tools should look like. Moreover, this shared concept changes through time from the corner notching of the Kirk type to the basal notching of the bifurcate types, yet the geographical distributions of these types vary insignificantly. It is tempting to speculate that this sharing of styles is reflective of a sharing of language. And, although archaeologists admonish that contemporary human societies often share styles and technologies across linguistic boundaries (Worth 2017), it may have been different for ancient hunter-gatherers on a sparsely populated landscape. Indeed, genetic studies provide

— 1 cm

Figure 2.14. Early Archaic Kirk Corner Notched spear points from Church Rockshelter No. 1.

evidence for the existence of a "macro–Siouan population, ancestral to Iroquoians, Siouans, and Caddoans, early in the prehistory of eastern North America" (Malhi et al. 2001:43). Perhaps this macro–Siouan genetic group is evidenced by the Kirk and bifurcate-type projectile points found from New England to Florida; their modern linguistic descendants include the Cherokees, who speak an Iroquoian language, and the Catawbas who speak a Siouan language.

The early Holocene hunter-gatherer adaptation manifested in and around the Appalachian Summit was evidently highly successful. Humans thrived in this stable, rich woodland environment and seasonally variable climate. If the numbers of sites and artifacts of this period are any indication, human populations were on the rise.

3

Middle Archaic Period: 6,000–3,000 BCE

Three young men were spending a couple of nights in a small rockshelter away from the main camp of their people. From this temporary station they would forage and hunt in the adjacent uplands, hoping to kill a bear, an elk or some deer. They awoke to a cool fall morning, just above freezing. A ray of sunlight escaped through a low gap in the ridge to the east, brightening the yellowing beech leaves. Their fire had barely kept them warm through the night by heating up the gneiss wall of the small shelter, but their muscles were stiff from sleeping in a cluster on the cold ground. They fed the fire with dry dead branches that they had snapped from the lower trunks of nearby hemlocks, and after warming their hands and feet, and after a breakfast of brook trout and chestnuts, they travelled up the river and into the wind to a shallow place where elk and deer regularly crossed. Large boulders on either side provided cover for the hunters, one stationed on either side of the river. The third circled uphill away from the river to flush deer into the trap. The hunters were armed with atlatls to propel spears tipped with white quartz points.

The hunt was, to say the least, an exercise in patience. The two behind the boulders sat perfectly still, listening and smelling the river-scented air more than watching. The mobile hunter trod uphill, away from the river, very slowly and silently, keeping the wind in his face and searching the ground for spoor or scat. After nearly three hours he heard a deer snort a warning to its peers to be watchful—that something wasn't right in the woods. The hunter could hear and smell that the group of deer was only the distance of a spear's throw ahead of him. He approached them in small advances, giving them only enough concern to be wary, never allowing himself to see the deer for fear that they would see him as well. Otherwise, they would thunder off in any direction rather than browse their way leisurely down to the river crossing where the other two hunters were waiting.

Boone Before Boone

Even above the gentle babbling of the river, the two could hear the movements of the deer through the leafy forest as they approached the crossing place. It sounded like a group of five or six. The deer stopped at the water's edge to listen, watch, and drink. Then the lone hunter burst into view to force the group to recklessly cross the shallows and come into view of the hunters waiting with their spears and spear throwers cocked. The first deer to cross was a large doe, perhaps five or six years old and weighing nearly two hundred pounds. Only one spear was propelled and it found her right lung. Her front legs buckled and she collapsed in the shallow water while the other four does fled up stream along the left bank. Before the fallen doe could regain her footing, the two hunters were upon her and cracked her skull with a cobble.

When the third hunter joined them, he carried by its tail a porcupine that he had speared when the fleeing deer had flushed it from a thicket. This would be their evening meal; porcupine was a rare delicacy for the hunters and its quills were valued for ornamentation and tattooing. That evening they sat between their fire and the shelter wall, relishing roasted porcupine and working on weaponry. The quartz point of the spear that had killed the deer had shattered and needed replacement. Over the fire its maker melted the pinesap glue by which the point's tapering base was affixed to the socketed hickory shaft. In removing the quartz base, he was careful to recover any adhering glue for attaching the new quartz point that he had fashioned the night before. A gentle rain mixed its fresh smells with those of the roasted meat, wood smoke, and farting men in the small shelter. By morning the deer meat wrapped in its hide would be ready for schlepping back to the three hungry families who were camped a few kilometers downriver.

******

By the Middle Archaic period the climate of the Southeastern United States had become warmer. The period of between 6,000 and 3,000 BCE is known as the mid–Holocene climatic optimum, Atlantic climatic interval, Altithermal interval, or middle part of the Hypsithermal climatic episode. Nevertheless, the average effect in northern latitudes was a long period of warmer, and in many places drier weather. To the west of the Appalachian Summit, the Prairie margin expanded eastward. To the South, and East, along the Coastal Plain, very little climatic or environmental change is evident for the period. Evidence of climatic change from within the Appalachian Summit is nearly lacking. But evidence of accelerated sedimentation from adjacent eastern Piedmont

3. Middle Archaic Period: 6,000–3,000 BCE

and VRP floodplain sites during the mid–Holocene suggests high runoff from stormy events in the mountains (Schuldenrien 1996).

The beginning of the Middle Archaic period in the southern Appalachian region is visibly recognized by subtle changes in the lives of hunter-gatherers. These changes are reflected in many ways, including technology, settlement patterns, and regional interaction. They were, in part, responses to the warming climate of the time, which is evident in changes in plant and animal communities and in geomorphology. In parts of the Southeast the warming was accompanied by wetter conditions, while in others, especially to the west of the Appalachian Summit, drier conditions prevailed.

The Middle Archaic period of the Appalachian Summit includes four phases marked by changes in projectile technologies:

Stanly/Kanawha: 6,000–5,000 BCE
Morrow Mountain: 5,000–4,000 BCE
Guilford: 4,200–3,500 BCE
Late Middle Archaic (Unnamed): 4,000–3,000 BCE

These date ranges are based on evidence from the stratified Cold Canyon site in Swain County, North Carolina (Shumate and Kimball 2016) and the Coontree site in Transylvania County, North Carolina (Shumate and Kimball 2006). The Middle Archaic Kirk Stemmed phase, defined by evidence from sites on the Piedmont of North Carolina (Coe 1964) is not well represented in the mountains, and the projectile points that define it are difficult to distinguish from Stanly type points in the region.

The Late Middle Archaic phase has only recently been recognized and has not been given a formal name. Excavations by ASU at the Cold Canyon and Coontree sites have identified an eight-hundred-year period represented by strata overlying those of the Morrow Mountain and Guilford phases but underlying that of the Appalachian Stemmed (Savannah River) phase (Shumate and Kimball 2016).

Stanly/Kanawha Phase

Represented by medium to large spear points with expanding stems and slight basal notches (Figure 3.1), the Stanly/Kanawha phase in the Appalachian Summit dates to between 6,000 and 5,000 BCE. The Stanly phase was named for Stanly County on the Piedmont of North Carolina.

Figure 3.1. Middle Archaic Stanly (left and center) and Kanawha (right) spear points

Recognizable only by its distinctive projectile points, the phase is not well represented in the Appalachian Summit. Stratified sites containing an abundance of evidence of preceding (Early Archaic) and succeeding (Morrow Mountain) occupations may yield only one or two Stanly projectile points. These are often made of Knox formation chert, banded Shady formation chalcedony, or Piedmont dacite. In the Great Smoky Mountains, they were made from locally abundant vein quartz and quartzite (Bass 1977).

Stanly type projectile points are found mostly to the east of the Appalachian Summit, but in small amounts to the west, in the VRP. The phase was named by Joffre Coe (1964) based on evidence from the stratified Doerschuk site in Montgomery County on the North Carolina Piedmont. The projectile points, undoubtedly spear or atlatl dart points, are very similar in form to Kanawha points. Stanly points, though, tend to be larger.

Kanawha type projectile points, first identified and named from evidence along the Kanawha River in West Virginia (Broyles 1971), are similar in age and form to Stanly points but have a more expanding base and a more western distribution (Figure 3.1). They are, on the average, larger than earlier bifurcate forms but also exhibit serrations and asymmetrical blades as a result of sharpening one edge more often than the other. The bases are only slightly bilobate as a result of a shallow basal notch (Figure 3.1). Kanawha points in the northern part of

3. Middle Archaic Period: 6,000–3,000 BCE

the Appalachian Summit are often made of yellow jasper or chalcedony, presumably derived from the Shady Formation of the VRP. Chert and quartz specimens are also common.

Morrow Mountain Phase

Named for Morrow Mountain, one of the highest peaks in the Uwharrie Mountains on the central Piedmont of North Carolina, the Morrow Mountain phase was originally defined by distinctive large projectile points with rounded, rather than notched bases (Figure 3.2). Coe (1964), based on evidence at the Doerschuk site, eight kilometers northeast of Morrow Mountain on the Yadkin River, delineated two subphases of the Morrow Mountain phase; Morrow Mountain I and Morrow Mountain II. The former, occurring below the latter in stratigraphy, is characterized by a triangular blade and a short, sometimes pointed stem, while the latter has a longer and narrower blade and a longer, more rounded base (Coe 1964).

In the Appalachian Summit, the Morrow Mountain phase dates to

Figure 3.2. Middle Archaic Morrow Mountain spear points.

between 5,000 and 4,000 BCE. Morrow Mountain type projectile points are common but tend to be much smaller than those from the type-site on the Piedmont and are difficult to separate into Coe's subtypes. They are most often made from locally abundant vein quartz, but occasionally are made from VRP chert and chalcedony, or from Mount Rogers rhyolite or Piedmont dacite. As is the case for the earlier Stanly points, Morrow Mountain artifacts are found throughout North Carolina and to a lesser extent in the bordering states to the north, west, and south.

The shift from notched spear points to ones with tapering stems indicates a change in the hafting mechanism. These spear points were probably glued into the hollowed ends of spear shafts or fore-shafts with a heat-soluble resin such as pinesap that would have facilitated very fast replacement of broken points during the hunt. This also may, in part, explain the shift to an emphasis on locally abundant but less tractable quartz in the manufacture of the points. With less investment in the lithic material, Morrow Mountain points would have been more expendable and thus replaced more often than the earlier notched points made of exogenous chert. If this is so, archaeologists must consider the fact that an increase in the numbers of Morrow Mountain points over earlier forms in the region cannot be taken as evidence of increasing human presence; there were simply more of them made and discarded.

Guilford Phase

Named for Guilford County, North Carolina, the Guilford phase was defined by Joffre Coe (1964) on the basis of a stratum at the Doerschuk site containing a predominance of large, thick, lanceolate spear points (Figure 3.3). Found stratigraphically above Morrow Mountain type projectile points at Doerschuk and at Cold Canyon (Shumate and Kimball 2016), this evidence is believed to date to between 4,200 and 3,500 BCE. No sites or strata containing strictly Guilford phase artifacts have been discovered in the Appalachian Summit. However, Guilford type spear points are commonly found throughout the region on a variety of landforms indicating a continued but seasonal presence of foragers in the uplands.

Like the preceding Morrow Mountain phase, Guilford points tend to be made on locally abundant but poorly tractable quartz, quartzite, and Mount Rogers rhyolite rather than the finer cryptocrystalline chert, chalcedony, and jasper from the VRP to the west. Indeed, tools of this

3. Middle Archaic Period: 6,000–3,000 BCE

Figure 3.3. Middle Archaic Guilford spear points.

phase are rarely found in the VRP, indicating that the western extent of the phase and possibly the territory occupied by its human representatives was the Blue Ridge physiographic province. This may indicate gradual territorial constrictions in the later part of the Middle Archaic period, perhaps influenced by human population growth and competition for resources in the overall Southeast.

Late Middle Archaic Phase

Excavations at the Coontree (Shumate and Kimball 2006) and Cold Canyon (Shumate and Kimball 2016) sites in the southwestern mountains of North Carolina provided evidence of a previously unrecognized late Middle Archaic phase represented by a variety of medium-sized stemmed projectile points, usually constructed of vein quartz or quartzite (Figure 3.4). These are virtually indistinguishable from ones of the Late Archaic (Iddins) and Early Woodland (Swannanoa and Ebenezer) periods, and were recognized as earlier forms only because they were found in a datable stratum overlying Morrow Mountain and Guilford phase deposits and underlying strata containing Late Archaic

Figure 3.4. Projectile points from late Middle Archaic contexts at the Cold Canyon site, Swain County, North Carolina (modified from Shumate and Kimball [2016]).

Appalachian Stemmed knives. This reminds us that projectile point shapes are not always reliable indicators of precise time periods. As they do today, some technologies remained effective for longer periods in the past than did others. Previously abandoned technological traits also may reappear in much later times if they become useful or adaptive again. A case in point is the side-notching of spear points in the Early Archaic period, thousands of years before the hafting technique reappears in the Late Archaic period.

Artifacts of the Middle Archaic Period

In addition to the projectile points discussed above, Middle Archaic period sites often include the usual suite of cobble tools (hammers, anvils, grinding stones, etc.), atlatl weights, and chipped stone flake tools of a variety of shapes and serving a variety of purposes, such as scraping, planing, sawing, and perforating (Figure 3.5). The latter differ significantly from the flake tools of the preceding Early Archaic and Paleoindian periods, which were more often made on large, long blades

3. Middle Archaic Period: 6,000–3,000 BCE

Figure 3.5. Middle Archaic flake tools from Church Rockshelter No. 1.

with parallel sides. Those more formalized blade tools were made to last and to be used extensively, while the flake tools of the Middle Archaic period were made on flakes of various shapes that were detached from amorphously shaped cores and from thinning bifaces. They can best be described as "expedient tools" that were discarded after one or two uses.

The distinctive atlatl weights of this period, usually constructed of soft rocks such as siltstone and soapstone, were chipped, ground, and then polished into symmetrical, often lunate shapes, with a hole drilled though the center for attachment (Figure 3.6). These represent the earliest known evidence of atlatls in the Southeast, although earlier perishable forms may not have incorporated stone weights. Stanly type atlatl weights, usually broken through the center hole, have been found on sites such as the Gwyn Hayes site (see below) in the Appalachian Summit. There is no evidence that bow-and-arrow technology had been introduced or developed in the Southeast until after the Middle Archaic period. Use of the atlatl indicates that most large-game hunting took place in clearings or at forest edges (wielding an atlatl to propel a spear in the forest is similar to swinging a golf club in the same setting). By extent, its priority in the hunting technology of the time suggests that there were extensive open spaces within the southeastern hardwood forests where the technology could be effective.

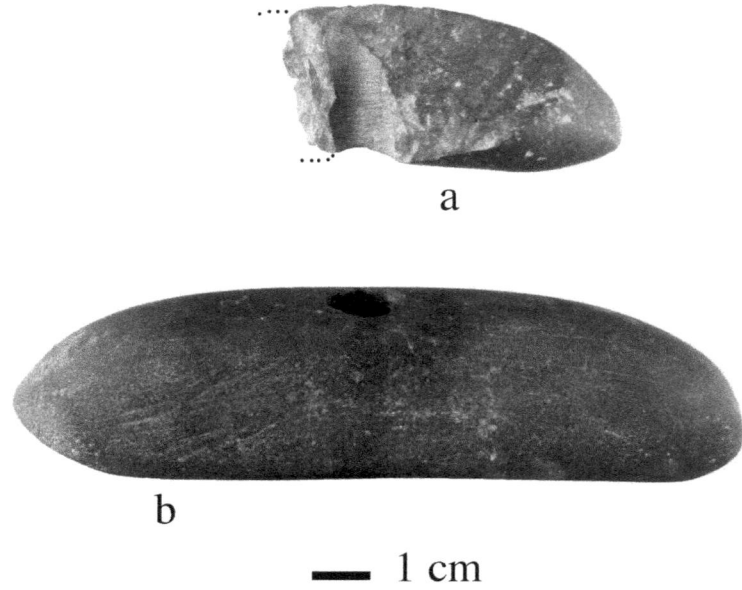

Figure 3.6. Middle Archaic Stanly atlatl weights.

Mountain Life in the Middle Archaic Period

We know from the scant evidence preserved over the millennia that humans in the Middle Archaic period of the Appalachian summit were seasonally migratory hunters and gatherers who visited the uplands mostly during seasons that would have provided their primary need, and that is food. Although most of the stone artifacts of this time period, especially in the Morrow Mountain phase, are made of quartz that is locally abundant, some are made of chert and chalcedony found in the VRP of eastern Tennessee and southwestern Virginia, some are made of Mount Rogers rhyolite found in southwestern Virginia, and some are made of dacite from the Piedmont of North Carolina. This suggests that migrants were moving through the higher valleys of the Appalachian Summit from various directions, possibly covering an area of 150 to 300 linear kilometers. They probably traveled in small groups of individual or related families along well-established pathways through gaps and along stream courses, camping at the same ideal sites year after year. These included open-air sites such as Gwyn Hayes, located within

3. Middle Archaic Period: 6,000–3,000 BCE

the Boone city limits (Whyte and Quick 1996), and rockshelters such as Church Rockshelter No. 1 (Whyte 2013b). At both sites, toolmakers fashioned Morrow Mountain spear points and other tools from white quartz cobbles obtained from nearby rivers and streams.

Another Middle Archaic site, Miller II, located on Howard's Creek just north of Boone, was excavated by Appalachian State University in the 1970s but never reported. Most of the temporally diagnostic tools recovered are Morrow Mountain points made of quartz or dacite. Other spear points include Middle Archaic Kanawha types made of chert (Figure 3.7 a) and crystal quartz (Figure 3.7 b & c), and a quartzite Guilford spear point (Figure 3.7 f). The site also yielded many pitted cobbles and hammer stones that may have been used for nut processing (Figure 3.7 g).

Middle Archaic sites with preserved food remains are very rare in the Appalachian Summit and thus far have been found only in rockshelters where organic preservation is better. Church Rockshelter No. 1, located along Watauga River near Valle Crucis, contained a Middle Archaic stratum that yielded several Stanly, Morrow Mountain, and Guilford type spear points as well as animal bones (Whyte 2013b). Remains of white-tailed deer, turkey, squirrel, turtles, snakes, and fish indicate hunting, collecting, and fishing for a variety of animal foods—a typical array for foraging societies. Also recovered were bones and teeth of American porcupine (*Erethizon dorsatum*), one of which was burnt. Two of these were radiocarbon dated to approximately 5,500 BCE, indicating that porcupines existed in the Appalachian Summit and were probably hunted and consumed by humans at the site in the Middle Archaic period (Whyte 2010b).

A study of Middle Archaic site distributions in the broader Southeast (Sassaman 2001) shows that the hunter-gatherers of the Morrow Mountain phase in the Appalachian Summit and to the east were small groups of foragers creating small campsites and resource extraction sites generally distributed across the landscape (also see Bass 1977), whereas their contemporaries west of the Appalachians created larger base camps along larger river courses that were occupied for longer periods. This and evidence of interpersonal conflict and participation in long-distance exchange indicate increasing cultural complexity in the Middle Archaic period to the west.

Little is known of the burial practices of Middle Archaic period humans. At one of the better-preserved sites of the time period, the Eva site in Benton County, Tennessee, nearly two hundred burials were

Figure 3.7. Spear points and pitted cobble from the Miller II site, Watauga County, North Carolina.

3. Middle Archaic Period: 6,000–3,000 BCE

excavated, seventeen of which are contemporaneous with the Morrow Mountain phase. These include burials of adult males and females and 1 two-year-old. Adults were buried in the flesh in a variety of positions, but mostly flexed and lying on their sides. The child was buried extended and supine as though bound to a cradleboard (Lewis and Lewis 1961). The only artifacts associated with these burials were a bone needle and a few bone beads. The skeletal remains were unusually well preserved because of overlying freshwater mollusk shell deposits that bolstered and stabilized calcium in the bone.

The Winklers Meadow Road Site

In spring and summer of 1992 ASU archaeologists excavated a small site next to Winkler Creek in Boone where an apartment building was to be constructed (Kimball and Whyte 1992). Most of the site's contexts had been disturbed by recent cultivation, but parts of hearths, consisting of clusters of burned rocks, remained intact. The only precontact artifacts recovered were ones made of stone—all others having perished. In addition to flakes of quartz, quartzite, rhyolite, and chert, several projectile points were found dating to various time periods. Most, however, are from the Middle Archaic period. These include five heavily patinated Stanly type spear points made of Piedmont dacite (Figure 3.8). Two of these evidently broke while in use; the other three had been sharpened (by flaking the edges) to the point of exhaustion.

Evidently, the site's occupants, a small hunting and gathering group, had migrated up from the Piedmont region sometime between 6,000 and 5,400 BCE. At the site they made hearths with cobble platforms for

Figure 3.8. Stanly spear points from the Winklers Meadow Road site, Boone, North Carolina.

roasting foods and to provide warmth and light, and engaged in "retooling." This involved replacing broken and exhausted spear points in the haft with new ones made at the site or carried with them for anticipated use. No flakes of the same dacite material were found on the site. This indicates that the points were replaced with ones already manufactured or ones made of locally abundant quartz or of non-lithic materials such as bone or antler.

When only stone artifacts remain preserved on a site like this there is a tendency to overlook the activities and even the possible presence of women. They may have busied themselves in food preparation, basketry, processing plant fibers, twisting cordage, net making, et cetera—industries involving perishable materials.

The Gwyn Hayes Site

On the eastern end of Boone, North Carolina, there is a bank, a pharmacy, and an ABC store. Before these were built there was a cluster of houses. Long before the houses were built Native Americans periodically camped there to avail themselves of the high, dry, and level ground, the vast view of the Boone Valley to the west where three streams converge to become the South Fork of the New River, and the various food resources that abounded in summer and fall. The site also was a hub for travel between the headwaters of the New, Watauga, and Yadkin Rivers. In 1993 part of the land that contained the site was advertised as the future site of a medical office complex (it was later sold and then a bank was built). Finding flakes of flint and quartz on an eroding surface at the edge of Hodges Street, the author got permission from the owner to engage the Appalachian State University Field Archaeology class in salvage excavations of the site (Whyte and Quick 1996). Two seasons of excavation in relatively undisturbed portions of the site (places where there had been no recent structures) revealed remarkably well-preserved contexts including hearths, and clusters of stone artifacts immediately beneath the sod (Figure 3.9).

Artifacts recovered include stone tools typologically dated to between 12,000 and 3,000 years ago. Wood charcoal from a cobble-lined hearth (Figure 3.10) was radiocarbon dated to 2,110–2,090 BCE. While the site was used many times in prehistory, much of the evidence dates to the Middle Archaic period—an abundance of quartz artifacts and projectile points of the Stanly and Morrow Mountain types (Figure 3.11). Although no food remains were found preserved on the site,

3. Middle Archaic Period: 6,000–3,000 BCE

Figure 3.9. The Gwyn Hayes site, Boone, North Carolina.

Figure 3.10. Late Archaic hearth at the Gwyn Hayes site, Boone, North Carolina.

evidence indicates brief seasonal occupations by small groups of hunters and gatherers who foraged and hunted in the surrounding valley and uplands. In the evenings, they probably prepared and consumed food, made new tools and replaced their broken or expended tools around the hearth. These seasonal occupations probably took place in late summer or fall when nuts were in abundance and white-tailed deer, elk, and black bear were prime for hunting.

The Cold Canyon Site

Located on a small tributary of the Little Tennessee River in Nantahala National Forest, Swain County, North Carolina, the Cold Canyon site was explored by ASU archaeologists from 1998 through 2001 (Shumate and Kimball 2016). Originally discovered by a cultural resource management survey in 1992 and described as an insignificant "lithic scatter," the site was re-investigated by archaeologist Scott Shumate, and determined to be an important stratified Archaic period camp site. Sediments gradually accumulating on the site from erosion of the adjacent steep slope, and intermittent occupation by humans between 6,000 and 1,000 BCE, resulted in nearly a meter of deposits and seven distinct strata from which over 100,000 stone artifacts, several metric tons of burned rocks, fired clay objects, and a smattering of carbonize plant and animal remains were recovered. Among the stone artifacts recovered were over 750 stone tools, including projectile points, scrapers, axes, grinding slabs, and anvils. Carbonized plant remains recovered by flotation and wet screening included wood charcoal and hickory nutshell. Animal remains, poorly preserved, include calcined fragments of deer, turkey, and turtle bone.

The site was evidently used by seasonally migratory people foraging the uplands for food resources and availing themselves of the abundant high-quality quartzite cobbles exposed in the adjacent creek. Site activities included stone tool manufacture, food processing and consumption, and hide scraping, among others (Shumate and Kimball 2016). Fragments of fired clay slabs with textile impressions were found in Late Archaic strata. These are similar in form to ones found in Early Archaic components at the Icehouse Bottom site in eastern Tennessee and Dust Cave in northern Alabama (Sherwood and Chapman 2005) and may have been parts of larger surfaces used in food preparation. Shumate and Kimball (2016) suggest, however, that the fired clay may have been

3. Middle Archaic Period: 6,000–3,000 BCE

technology associated with the intentional thermal alteration of quartzite—a possible benefit to the systematic fracturing (knapping) of the stone to form tools.

A rare example of a stratified site in the southern Appalachians, Cold Canyon has provided one of the only views of technological change through time in the Middle and Late Archaic periods for the region and has served to tighten our chronologies for the period. Seven radiocarbon dates ranging between 5,340 and 3,580 BCE and associated with distinctive clusters of projectile point types were derived from samples of carbonized plant material. The vertical distribution of projectile point types throughout the site's profile revealed some surprises. Archaeologists working in the Appalachian Summit, perhaps too regularly, refer to projectile point sequences observed at stratified sites in neighboring regions, especially the Piedmont Plateau to the east (e.g., Coe 1964), when identifying point types and estimating ages of sites from them. Indeed, a few of the types identified by Coe (1964) and others, such as the Guilford, Morrow Mountain, and Savannah River types, were found in great numbers and in expected vertical order at Cold Canyon. These indicated use of the site beginning in the Middle Archaic Morrow Mountain phase and extending through the Middle Archaic Guilford phase and the Late Archaic Savannah River (or Appalachian Stemmed) phase.

Note, however, the time gap of over 1,000 years between the end of the Guilford phase and the beginning of the Late Archaic period; this gap was represented by Zones G and H, which contained much archaeological evidence, including a variety of medium-sized projectile points with either tapered, straight, or expanding stems for hafting (Figure 3.4). Similar types were observed stratigraphically between Morrow Mountain and Late Archaic types at sites in the adjacent Valley and Ridge province (Chapman 1975, 1977, 1978, 1979) but not named. Overlapping in form and material composition with later types such as Iddins (Chapman 1981), Ebenezer (Kneberg 1956) and Swannanoa (Keel 1976), these projectile points would be difficult to identify as belonging to the Middle Archaic period if found on the surface.

Summary

The Middle Archaic period, lasting for nearly three thousand years, appears to have been a period of relative stability for the native residents of the southern Appalachian region. Aside from minor changes in stone technologies, we see little evidence of change in human life throughout the period. Small, egalitarian hunting and gathering groups foraged in the mountains and the surrounding lowlands, making moves according to seasonal changes in food resource availability. The sites tend to be small camps placed on terraces, toe slopes, ridges, and alluvial fans near springheads. There are indications of gradual population increase in this period that ultimately would result in more territorial restriction and development of regional exchange in subsequent periods. One indication is that Guilford type projectile points show a slightly more restricted distribution than their Morrow Mountain predecessors. Another indicator is that Middle Archaic stone tools are made primarily of stone acquired from close to the sites on which they are found, suggesting limited access to perhaps more desirable lithic materials (such as chert) controlled by other humans.

4.

Late Archaic Period: 3,000 to 1,000 BCE

Under her mother's tutelage, she pecked and pecked at the soft soapy blue-gray rock with a handheld quartzite pick that she had made from a river cobble. With every impact, small bits of rock dust would explode from the surface. Her goal was to shape this large nodule of soapstone into a thin-walled vessel with lug handles for boiling nutmeats and making bread. She and the other women working at the quarry site that day chanted as they pecked, singing a song about the ivory billed woodpecker, whose staccato pecking in the giant oaks and chestnuts was mimicked by their own industry. On a previous visit to the site she had hacked at the large outcropping to isolate a mushroom-shaped nodule, and then broke it away from the bedrock with a lever consisting of a large white oak branch. For several months the nodule lay hidden in the creek, awaiting her return to finish it. Hollowing the nodule with her pick was tedious and made her very anxious; the closer she got to finishing the vessel, the more delicate it became. Too many were the times that her mother and aunts had broken vessels in the process of making them. Indeed, the ground around her was littered with the evidence.

Working at the soapstone quarry was a welcomed break in the monotony of a typical day at her residential camp. Her daily tasks included gathering firewood, tending the hearth, gathering seeds, nuts, roots, and anything that crawled in the forest or field. She also collected mountain cane, milkweed, and the inner bark of poplar trees, and from these made mats, baskets, cordage, clothing, and nets. Other women did all these things and nursed babies and minded children. It occurred to her that she works a lot harder than the young men in her tribe; their sole responsibility was making and maintaining weaponry and killing animals and other humans. Then, they'd sit around the fire in the evening and talk about killing. The thorn under her fingernail reminded her that before coming to the soapstone quarry she and the other women and children had gathered in a line at the base of a steep slope of chestnut trees where they had burned away the fallen leaves to expose fallen, scorched chestnuts. As they ascended the slope they filled baskets with the nuts, which were easily separated from their scorched spiny hulls, though sometimes their fingers would get pierced. Further roasting them killed most of the worms that had bored into the nuts and made it so they could be stored for winter consumption. The people learned from the squirrels that the nuts could be stored underground.

After half a day of hollowing the vessel and roughly shaping its handles, the young woman soothed her burning hands and elbow in the cold creek below where the group was working. Following a snack of dried meat and chestnut bread, she prepared for the next part of the process. For this she had brought to the site a grinding pebble of very coarse sandstone and a hand-sized flake of tough quartzite with a steeply angled, rounded edge for scraping the vessel interior. Alternately scraping and abrading the interior and exterior, the vessel, after several more hours of her labor, took on its final form. The final smoothing was then accomplished with a small pebble of fine-grained sandstone.

She was proud of her first vessel. It was strong yet thin, smooth, and symmetrical. With great care, it would serve her, her husband-to-be, and the family they would have for many years to come. Although it weighed as much as small child, she would strap it to her back in a leather bag and carry it to the various places they would reside. The vessel would be a constant fixture at the fire for boiling nuts and meats. It also would serve as an oven to bake acorn and chestnut loaves by inverting it over a hot flat stone and covering it with hot coals. That is why she was careful to isolate the opposing lug handles slightly below the vessel rim. For her people, cooking bread in this way was an active metaphor for gestation and creating life.

Some of the vessels that the other women were making would be exchanged for things that they needed but were not to be found within their territorial range. They owned the soapstone, but others had better access to the precious marine shell beads that adorned their wrists and necks and gave them protection and reminded them of the cycle of life and death. So valuable were the vessels they made that some would be exchanged and gifted along a chain of human alliances that reached as far as the lower Mississippi valley and peninsular Florida.

******

4. Late Archaic Period: 3,000–1,000 BCE

The warmer and drier period of the middle Holocene Epoch in the Southeast came to an end at approximately 3,000 BCE. Across the Southeast river channels had begun to stabilize, creating terrace systems and riverine resources that became the focus of Late Archaic period human settlement in the lowlands (Schuldenrein 1996). The archaeological record of this period in the mountains is extensive and, if the dramatic increase in the numbers and sizes of sites are any indication, human populations flourished during this wetter period. Large settlements along the major eastern tributaries of the Mississippi River, such as the Tennessee, Cumberland, Ohio, and Greene rivers included architecture, cemeteries, and sometimes mounds of freshwater mollusk shell. Large settlements have also been noted for the primary river valleys of the southeastern Coastal Plain where ceramic technology first appeared during this period. The Appalachian Summit, however, remained a place of seasonal visitation, but with a significantly increased human presence, probably because of its possession of valuable lithic resources—notably soapstone, greenstone, and quartzite. Because of these materials, the Appalachian Summit, possibly for the first time, played a key role in exchange of technological, ornamental, and ritual paraphernalia throughout the Southeast.

There are several technologies that are considered markers for the Late Archaic period in the mountains. These include medium sized stemmed and notched projectile points, large stemmed stone knife blades, grooved axe heads usually made from greenstone, and soapstone vessels. The earliest projectile point types of the Late Archaic period in the mountains are medium to large side-notched forms with excurvate blades and heavily ground bases and notches (Figure 4.1). They are often made of quartzite, vein quartz, and rhyolite, and are assignable to the Brewerton Side Notched type defined by William Ritchie (1940) from evidence at the Brewerton site in New York. Earlier researchers in the region appear to have mistaken these for similar Early Archaic notched spear points, but the Brewerton type is distinctive and is found from New England to the southern Appalachians, indicating that occupants of the entire mountain chain were at least a community of practice in the sharing of technological styles.

Later projectile points of this period include Iddins, Ledbetter, Otarre, Small Appalachian Stemmed, and Lamoka types (Figure 4.2). These are all medium to large stemmed forms. Iddins type points were defined based on evidence from the Iddins site in Loudoun County, Tennessee (Chapman 1981). They have a mean length of about 45 mm,

Figure 4.1. Late Archaic Brewerton spear points.

and straight to slightly expanding stems that are usually "unfinished" at the base (Figure 4.2 b). This means that the bases often exhibit either the weathered cortex or the flat striking platform remaining on the proximal end of the flake blank used to make the projectile point. This is also characteristic of the Lamoka type defined by Ritchie (1932) (Figure 4.2 c). Like the earlier Brewerton points, Lamoka points are found throughout the Appalachian chain.

Similarly, the Otarre points defined by Keel (1976) from findings

Figure 4.2. Late Archaic stemmed projectile points: (a) Small Appalachian Stemmed (b) Iddins (c) Lamoka (d) Ledbetter/Otarre.

4. Late Archaic Period: 3,000–1,000 BCE

in terminal Late Archaic period strata at the Warren Wilson site in Buncombe County, North Carolina, are virtually indistinguishable from the Ledbetter type (Figure 4.2 d) that had been described by Kneberg (1956). They have slightly tapering stems, asymmetrical blades, and in the Appalachian Summit are most often made of a distinctive blue-gray bedded chert (Whyte 2014). The asymmetry of the blade suggests that they functioned as knives rather than as projectile points.

Artifacts of the Late Archaic Period

Archaeologists identify Late Archaic sites in the Appalachian Summit by the presence of distinctive and non-perishable stone artifacts such as soapstone vessels, large stemmed knife blades, grooved axe blades, and bell-shaped pestles probably used for seed grinding. The knife blades, traditionally called Appalachian Stemmed or Savannah River "points," are usually made of quartzite or rhyolite, measure up to 20 cm in length, and have squared, rounded, or slightly concave stems for hafting (Figure 4.3). The large blades are often heavily worn on the edges, were asymmetrically sharpened (Figure 4.4), and rarely exhibit impact fractures at the tip. These characteristics and their overall dimensions indicate their primary function as knives rather than spear points (Whyte 2014). Until one is found preserved in its haft or until they are subjected to extensive studies of use-wear,

— 1 cm

Figure 4.3. Late Archaic Appalachian Stemmed knives.

Figure 4.4. Asymmetrically sharpened Appalachian Stemmed knives.

hafting-wear, breakage, and context, their precise functions will remain hypothetical.

Appalachian Stemmed knives occur in great numbers and on many sites in the Appalachian Summit and, albeit with other appellations, throughout the eastern United States. They appear to have been introduced to the Late Archaic tool kit in the southeastern lowlands around 5,000 BCE and then spread among societies westward and northward by means of diffusion and sometimes population displacement (Sassaman 2001). In the Appalachian Summit, they range in age between 3,000 and 1,600 BCE (Chapman 1981; GAI Consultants, Inc. 1986). One was recovered from a large feature that may have been a burial at the Bynum Taylor site just downriver from Valle Crucis, North Carolina. Charcoal from the same feature was radiocarbon dated to about 1,850 BCE (Purrington 1983). The co-occurrence of these knives with the earliest evidence of horticulture in the region may indicate a functional relationship (e.g., plant harvesting/processing). But they also resemble the large knives of the same period in California where they are similarly found in association with a mast-forest adaptation and interpreted as evidence of males competing for prestige in big-game hunting as a response to increases in human population, emphasis on high-cost subsistence resources (acorns), and the increasing importance of women's roles in subsistence (Hildebrandt and McGuire 2002).

During the first half of the Late Archaic, when the large knives

4. Late Archaic Period: 3,000–1,000 BCE

supplied the cutting edges, smaller stemmed and side notched objects may have functioned as projectile tips. Another possibility is that some spears or arrows at that time were tipped with sharp wood, bone, or antler, which, unfortunately, are perishable materials that seldom survive the moist acidic soils of the southern mountains. Antler points were found in abundance in Middle and Late Archaic strata at the famous Eva site along the Tennessee River in Benton County, Tennessee (Lewis and Lewis 1961) and at Indian Knoll in Ohio County, Kentucky (Webb 1974) where calcium in the soil was stabilized by the abundance of mollusk shells. Perhaps the use of antler projectile points was widespread in the mid Holocene. The later part of the Late Archaic period witnessed the phasing out of the large stemmed knives and the appearance of smaller stemmed knives such as the Ledbetter (or Otarre) types, which were coeval with Iddins and Lamoka projectile points. Toward the end of the Late Archaic period, utilitarian functions of the large stemmed knives may have been met by simple flake tools with long cutting edges.

Atlatls were certainly in use in the Southern Appalachians in the Late Archaic, although few remains of them have been recovered. Probable atlatl parts discovered within the region include so-called "banner stones" which may have functioned as atlatl weights (Figure 4.5). These are winged and drilled objects carved from soft stone, which, if attached near the hook of the atlatl, would have provided additional forward momentum. Parts of atlatls, including handles, weights, and hooks, have been recovered from sites in the broader Southeast having better preservation and contexts. For example, at Indian Knoll in Kentucky several graves included the handles, weights, and hooks of atlatls aligned in ways that indicated their composition.

Many researchers argue that bow-and-arrow technology was introduced to the Southeast in the Late Archaic period (e.g., Bradbury 1997 and Whyte 2007a). The evidence consists of narrower projectile points, having narrower stems for hafting. Morphologies of projectile points such as the Lamoka type, which dates to between 3,500 and 2,500 BCE, statistically cluster with points known to have tipped arrows rather than spears (Whyte 2007a). Furthermore, the nock end of a cane arrow (reported in the following chapter) was found at the very bottom of the stratigraphy on the Early Woodland period (ca. 1,000 BCE) Camp Creek site in northeastern Tennessee, indicating the presence of the technology in the area by that time (Lewis and Kneberg 1957). The existence of the bow-and-arrow within the region in the Late Archaic implies the

Figure 4.5. Late Archaic atlatl weights.

possibility of increased warfare resulting from competition over territories, resources, and status. The bow-and-arrow would have conferred an advantage in warfare because of increased accuracy, more rapid firing, and the capacity of the archer to carry more projectiles (Bradbury 1997). Use of the atlatl and spears, especially in hunting large game, may have persisted well beyond the adoption of the bow-and-arrow (Bradbury 1997). The bow, as opposed to the atlatl, also is more effective hunting technology in the forest. Toward the end of the Late Archaic period, when this technology was adopted in the southern Appalachian region, people had begun to systematically burn forest understory to encourage growth of herbaceous annuals and fire tolerant oak and chestnut trees and possibly to attract browsers such as deer and grazers such as elk (Delcourt and Delcourt 1997). There may have been a decline in populations of elk and other grazers by 4,000 years ago, causing hardwood forests to expand and encouraging shifts in hunting technologies and the use of fire to "promote a heterogeneous mosaic of different vegetation types" (Delcourt and Delcourt 1997:1013).

Grooved axe heads made by pecking and grinding cobbles of various metamorphic rocks such as greenstone are a relatively common component of the Late Archaic tool kit (Figure 4.6). Their primary function was heavy woodworking such as felling trees, but they were also recycled into quarrying and digging tools. They occur in two broad morphological categories: full-grooved and three quarter-grooved. The latter morph is more common in the Appalachian region and exhibits

4. Late Archaic Period: 3,000–1,000 BCE

greater variation in form (Sassaman 1996). Their relative abundance may indicate the building of more permanent structures, forest clearing for gardening, and the approach of more sedentary habitation.

Other stone items common on Late Archaic sites include mortars and pestles for grinding seeds

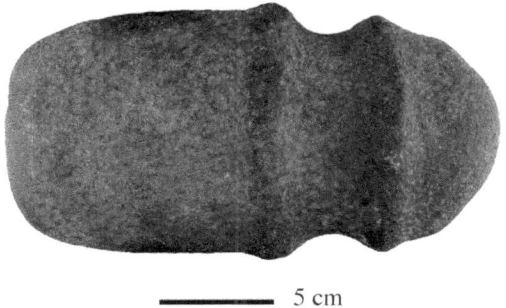

Figure 4.6. Late Archaic grooved axe.

(Figure 4.7) and so-called "nutting stones" (Figure 4.8). The latter are cobbles, slabs, or blocks of rock exhibiting one or more pits or "cupules" (pronounced "kyoopyools") that presumably held nuts while they were cracked with a hammer stone. Sometimes the cupules are arranged to represent star clusters such as the Pleiades (Figure 4.8), which held a special place in Native American cosmology (Lankford 2007; Whyte and Johnson 2013). That cupules frequently were laboriously pecked into the surfaces of boulder and bedrock petroglyphs in the Appalachian Summit (Loubser et al. 2019) suggests that many portable "nutting stones" containing similar cupules may have served other purposes

Figure 4.7. Late Archaic mortar (left) and pestle (right).

Figure 4.8. Nutting stone with cupules resembling the Pleiades (left) and with visible stars of the asterism superimposed (right).

or were made for other, perhaps symbolic reasons (Whyte and Johnson 2013). If they did function as nutting stones, they complement the evidence of increased reliance on nut products in the Late Archaic period (Whyte 2007a).

The development of a soapstone vessel industry at approximately 1,700 BCE, at the very end of the Late Archaic period, had a profound impact on human subsistence and socioeconomic life throughout the Eastern States. Soapstone, also called "steatite," is talc-rich metamorphic rock found throughout the eastern Piedmont and Blue Ridge provinces. Between 1,700 and 500 BCE soapstone cooking vessels were manufactured and distributed as much as 500 kilometers, to the Atlantic and Gulf coasts and the lower Mississippi valley. Source quarries located in the Appalachian Summit include the Blue Rock Soapstone Quarry in Yancey County, North Carolina (see below) and various sites near Spruce Pine, Todd, and West Jefferson, North Carolina. At these sites, soapstone outcrops were chiseled with stone and antler tools to isolate large nodules that could be pried off and reduced to unfinished but relatively portable vessel preforms (Figure 4.9). Vessels finished at nearby residential sites are often very large, heavy, (more than 10 kilograms) and kettle-shaped, some with opposing lug handles near the rim (Figure 4.10). Sometimes vessels were decorated with geometric incisions.

The frequent association of soapstone vessel fragments with hearths and the presence of carbonized residues (i.e., soot) on the exterior surfaces indicate that the vessels functioned primarily as cooking utensils, likely used in the boiling of mast (acorns, chestnuts, walnuts, and hickory nuts) (Truncer 2004). They also may have served in the

4. Late Archaic Period: 3,000–1,000 BCE

fashion of today's Dutch ovens, the likes of which (albeit for clay pottery) was observed by William Henry Timberlake in the 1750s (Williams 1948: 57) among the Overhill Cherokee:

> After making a fire on the hearth-stone, about the size of a large dish, they sweep the embers off; this they cover with a sort of deep dish, and renew the fire upon the whole, under which the bread bakes to as great perfection as in any European oven.

Figure 4.9. Soapstone vessel preform.

The thermal properties of soapstone are ideally suited to these purposes; it will not crack when exposed to extreme heat.

During the final phases of soapstone use in the northern Appalachian Region, extending into the subsequent Early Woodland period (700 BCE), soapstone vessels were also used as cremation urns, indicating the potentially important role of soapstone in ideology and ethnic identity. One cremation burial in a soapstone vessel was recovered from

Figure 4.10. Soapstone vessel from Mecklenburg County, North Carolina (courtesy of the Research Laboratories of Archaeology, University of North Carolina at Chapel Hill).

an undisclosed location in the Appalachian Summit of North Carolina in the 1990s, indicating strong cultural ties between the northernmost and southernmost portions of the Appalachian Chain.

Evidence from the Cold Canyon site in Swain County, North Carolina, indicates that prepared clay surfaces similar to those observed on Early and Middle Archaic sites such as Icehouse Bottom in Tennessee and Dust Cave in Alabama (Sherwood and Chapman 2005) may have been used in the Late Archaic period as well. Fragments of fired clay exhibiting textile impressions were found there in Late Archaic strata (Shumate and Kimball 2016). These may represent foundations of knowledge that led to the development of ceramic vessel technologies in the subsequent Early Woodland period.

Copper weaponry, tools, and ornaments were made and distributed from the Great Lakes region in the Late Archaic period but have yet to be discovered on sites of that age in the Appalachian Summit. However, a Late Archaic period human burial in a rockshelter in nearby eastern Kentucky included copper objects (Fiegel et al. 1992).

Mountain Life in the Late Archaic Period

While the lowlands surrounding the Appalachian Summit witnessed some degree of sedentary village life by the beginning of the Late Archaic period, no evidence of such (permanent structures, very large sites) has been discovered at elevations above 1,500 feet. Late Archaic sites in the Appalachian Summit are found on every type of landform, from flood plains to ridgetops, in rock shelters and in the open, and include seasonal base camps, quarry sites, and hunting stands. More intensive use of valley floors and margins over the preceding Middle Archaic is indicated by settlement data from the Great Smoky Mountains (Bass 1977). Furthermore, base camps such as Stratton Meadows and Iddins, discussed below, showed evidence of more prolonged and repeated occupation. Were these sites the result of seasonal use of the uplands by sedentary or semisedentary groups residing outside the Appalachian Summit? Or was there a resident population of migratory hunter-gatherers territorially restricted and adapted to the uplands? Evidence of territorial circumscription in much of the Southeast by the Late Archaic, and geographic restriction of typological markers such as the Iddins points support the latter.

A settlement pattern noted for the northern Appalachian region

4. Late Archaic Period: 3,000–1,000 BCE

(Versaggi et al. 2001), observes four major site groupings: base camps, multitask forager camps, resource processing locations, and single task field camps. This is seen as evidence of:

> ... hunter-gatherers with logistically organized systems of settlement, taking advantage of seasons when food resources aggregated, such as when deer congregate in fall and winter, and spawning fish run in the spring and fall. Residential base camps, tethered near these areas of concentrated resources form the core of the settlement system.... Specialized work groups ranged beyond the base, procuring and processing needed resources at overnight field camps. Closer to the residential base, daily foraging parties traveled to key areas to produce food and materials that easily could be transported back to the base in a day [Versaggi et al. 2001:132].

The Appalachian Summit, having similar topography and resource distributions, may also be characterized in this way but with one possible exception. If domesticated herbaceous annuals played a role in subsistence and settlement as they did in the adjacent lowlands and Cumberland Plateau (e.g., Gremillion 1996), prolonged occupation of summer base camps for the maintenance and harvesting of these resources may have been necessary. Cultivated plants, however, may qualify as a seasonally aggregated resource in the above model.

Indeed, the Late Archaic residents may have been the first of the region's practitioners of horticulture—the small-scale gardening of domesticated plants. Herbaceous annuals such as maygrass (*Phalaris caroliniana*), sumpweed (*Iva annua*), and goosefoot (*Chenopodium berlandieri*) were domesticated from indigenous wild varieties to produce plants with more and larger seeds, and seeds with thinner testa for human consumption. Sunflower (*Helianthus annuus*), pepo squash (*Cucurbita pepo*), and bottle gourd (*Lagenaria siceraria*) also were domesticated by Late Archaic times. The process of domestication was gradual and may, in part, have been accidental. The gathering, processing, and consumption of wild plant resources at spring and summer-season base camps would have resulted in the frequent deposition of select viable seeds in the disturbed soils (cleared and naturally fertilized) of habitation margins. The healthy plants emerging from the garbage heaps the following spring would have benefited the returning humans in their cyclical migration. Thus, a symbiosis evolved between humans and plants (see Rindos 1980). Intentional selection and planting of seeds from the more prolific or otherwise preferable seed producers would naturally follow, thus initiating the process of domestication.

Palynologists exploring the pollen and charcoal deposits in upland bogs and ponds of the Southern Appalachian region have discovered increased evidence of anthropogenic burning of the forest understory by approximately 1,000 BCE (Delcourt et al. 1998). This burning resulted not only in the clearing of understory for the purposes of gardening; it encouraged the growth of fire-tolerant oaks and American chestnut—important food sources.

In addition to carbonized seeds of domesticated plants, the associated processing technology (mortars and pestles) is found on many habitation sites in the region. Bell-shaped pestles of quartzite, laboriously pecked and ground into shape, are testimony to the importance of the new horticultural products in human subsistence. Wild plant foods and medicines evident in the archaeobotanical record for this period include wild forms of the aforementioned herbaceous annuals, nuts (especially acorn and black walnut), and wild grape (Chapman and Shea 1981).

The meat component of the Appalachian Summit residents in the Late Archaic period was likely focused on white-tailed deer but included many available edible vertebrates and invertebrates. Unfortunately, the poor preservation of animal remains in the uplands, again, precludes any detailed reconstructions of the meat diet. Late Archaic period strata at Eastman Rockshelter in extreme northeastern Tennessee yielded remains of white-tailed deer, elk, eastern box turtle, redhorse sucker, and freshwater drum (Manzano 1985). Many researchers have suggested that net sinkers, burned rock clusters, and even "broadpoints" (large stemmed knives) on Late Archaic base camps in eastern North America are indications of intensive fishing and fish meat processing (e.g., Chapman 1981; Turnbough 1975).

Due, in part, to preservation bias, Late Archaic period human remains are rare in the Appalachian Summit and immediate surrounds. Those yet discovered are exclusively the remnants of cremations, occurring on seasonal residences such as the Iddins site and in cemeteries such as the Kimberly-Clark site, both in the VRP of eastern Tennessee (Chapman 1990). The 28 cremations at Kimberly-Clark include primarily adults, both male and female, and date to approximately 1,032 BCE. The demographic composition of the cemetery and the presence of utilitarian items such as projectile points and flake tools among the remains reflect an egalitarian social organization. Chapman (1990:27) offers the hypothesis that "at least for the heart of the Great Valley, cremation was the preferred treatment of human remains during the Late Archaic period." In fact, this appears to be the case for the entire Appalachian region (Whyte 2007a).

4. Late Archaic Period: 3,000–1,000 BCE

Subsistence, settlement, and burial data for the Appalachian Summit between 4,000 and 1,000 BCE clearly represent egalitarian groups organized through kinship. The residents were seasonally migratory hunters-gatherers-fishers-gardeners whose dead were cremated and buried with items and in contexts suggestive of equal status and equal access to material resources. Although the resident societies appear to have been involved in regional economic exchange and conflict, there is no evidence of the existence of non-egalitarian social structures. These would develop later as resident populations graduated more toward sedentary village life, a greater emphasis on gardening, and increased interaction, either friendly or volatile, with more complex societies in adjacent lowlands.

The Wakeman II Site, Watauga County, North Carolina

Next to a springhead at an elevation of 4,200 feet, the Wakeman II site was explored by ASU archaeologists in 1976 and 1977 prior to its destruction by house construction. Purrington (1983:129) describes the site as "literally a quartzite pavement. Thousands of quartzite flakes, flake tools, and an occasional Savannah River point occur in the top few inches of soil over much of the site." This is remarkable considering that the site is estimated to be 65 kilometers and 900 vertical meters from the nearest quartzite source—the Erwin formation in eastern Tennessee. Indeed, none of the thousands of flakes exhibits any cortex (the weathered surface of the parent rock) and most of the flakes are large bifacial thinning flakes (Figure 4.11). This indicates that many large bifaces that had been formed at the quarry site were transported over a long distance to be finished at Wakeman II, either for use by their makers or for exchange. The finished products were clearly Appalachian Stemmed ("Savannah River") knives such as those found at the site (Figure 4.12c). Also recovered were Brewerton Side Notched points and small stemmed (Iddins/Lamoka) projectile points (Figure 4.12), hammer stones, anvil stones, and carbonized walnut and hickory nutshells (Purrington 1983).

Figure 4.11. Quartzite bifacial thinning flakes from the Wakeman II site, Watauga County, North Carolina.

Figure 4.12. Appalachian Stemmed knives and projectile points from the Wakeman II site, Watauga County, North Carolina.

4. Late Archaic Period: 3,000–1,000 BCE

The Stratton Meadows (Graham County, North Carolina) and Iddins (Loudoun County, Tennessee) Sites

The Stratton Meadows site is located in Stratton Gap on the North Carolina–Tennessee line at an elevation of just over 4,000 ft. Excavations in preparation for highway construction revealed a very large seasonal base camp with many fire pits and burned rock clusters. Radiocarbon dates on charcoal from these features suggest primary occupation between 1,900 and 1,700 BCE (GAI Consultants, Inc. 1986), which is the later part of the Late Archaic period, immediately preceding the development of the soapstone vessel industry in the Appalachian region. Most of the projectile points from the site were assigned to the Iddins undifferentiated narrow stemmed variety as defined by Chapman (1981) at the type-site in nearby Loudoun County, Tennessee.

The Iddins site, located on a first terrace of the Little Tennessee River at an elevation of only 750 ft., also contained a string of large pit features with burned rocks and carbonized wood and nutshell. Dates from this site range between 1,700–1,260 BCE (immediately post-dating Stratton Meadows). Unlike Stratton Meadows, the Iddins site excavations yielded hundreds of net sinkers (Figure 4.13); only one was found at Stratton Meadows. Iddins, probably because it was occupied a bit later in the Archaic period, also produced hundreds of fragments of soapstone vessels whereas none was recovered from Stratton Meadows. Otherwise, the two sites are remarkably similar in their overall structure and content, despite their extreme difference in elevation. No faunal remains are reported from either site. The carbonized plant remains from Stratton Meadows have yet to be analyzed. Those from the Iddins site include nut fragments of hickory, acorn, and especially walnut and butternut. Wild grape,

Figure 4.13. Late Archaic net sinkers.

sunflower, squash, gourd, and goosefoot were also represented (Chapman 1981). The unusual abundance of walnut shells at Iddins was considered anomalous. Their presence, however, might fit well with Chapman's interpretation of the site as a place of fishing and fish processing (Chapman 1981:148). Ethnohistorical accounts of southeastern native fishing often cite the use of poison derived from mashed walnut hulls or bark (e.g., Speck 1946). Juices from the hulls are also good sources of dye.

Blue Rock Soapstone Quarry, Yancey County, North Carolina

At an elevation of 2,720 feet and overlooking the Toe River in Yancey County, North Carolina, the Blue Rock Soapstone Quarry site provides a classic example of Late Archaic soapstone quarrying and vessel production (Mathis 1982). The soapstone source is a hump of material outcropping from the forest floor to a height of about one meter. Although much of the quarrying evidence at the site had been disturbed or defaced by road construction and modern quarrying of soapstone for crafts and construction, the outcrop still bore scars of ancient chiseling and many of the tools and byproducts of ancient quarrying were recovered by archaeological investigations.

Quarrying at the site was undertaken by isolating promontories on the outcrop by hacking or chiseling a circular trough with cobble tools and possibly recycled grooved axes. Once isolated, the mushroom-shaped nodule (vessel preform) was broken away by means of a wedge or lever, resulting in the creation of adjacent promontories for further quarrying. The acquired nodules were reduced and hollowed on site, by further pecking and chiseling, until they were deemed portable and to insure successful completion prior to export. Many production failures such as split nodules and broken vessel "rough-outs" are found on soapstone quarry sites, whereas the fragments of completed vessels are more common at residential bases such as the Iddins site.

Summary

The earliest evidence of involvement of the Appalachian Summit region in socio-economic interaction with surrounding regions emerges

4. Late Archaic Period: 3,000–1,000 BCE

in the Late Archaic period. Foundations of these interactions, whether involving trade, transhumance, or marriage, were established by the late Middle Archaic (circa 4,000 BCE) in larger river valleys of the lower elevations (Jeffries 1996). In the greater Southeast, marine shell objects and Great Lakes region copper artifacts are found on sites along the Green River of Kentucky (Jeffries 1996), artifacts of Appalachian or Piedmont region soapstone are found in peninsular Florida, the lower Mississippi valley, and southeastern Atlantic Coast (Sassaman 2001), and large knives of North Carolina Piedmont dacite are found on sites over 160 kilometers to the south (Goodyear et al. 1990). Territorial circumscription and sedentism in the lowlands precluded free access to needed resources and contributed to a need for alliances maintained through exchange of valuable objects and materials. The result may have been establishment of trade partners who gained status by way of their esoteric knowledge and access to exotic materials (Jeffries 1996).

Residents of the Appalachian Summit undoubtedly participated in regional exchange systems of the larger Southeast. Materials abundant in or restricted to the Appalachian Summit that may have been of value in surrounding territories during the Late Archaic include Mount Rogers formation rhyolite and Erwin formation quartzite for the making of large knives, greenstone for manufacture of grooved axes, and soapstone for the making of cooking vessels and other objects. The region was also rich in certain food resources, such as deer, black bear, chestnuts, and medicinal plants, which may have been exchanged extensively but left nothing in the way of archaeological evidence.

The archaeological facts of the Late Archaic period in the Appalachian Summit thus far collectively evince human population growth, territorial conscription, cooperative (economic) and competitive (warfare) interaction with adjacent regions, and moderate change in subsistence and settlement. In the preceding millennia of the Middle Archaic, the Appalachian Summit appears to have been a place of more seasonal use by wide-ranging, migratory hunter-gatherers who resided in the adjacent lowlands of the Piedmont and VRP. At that time, the Appalachian Summit was more of a frontier between the more sedentary river-adapted societies of the interior and more migratory foraging groups to the east (Sassaman 2001). In the Late Archaic, however, the region may have hosted its own alpine-adapted residents with a more restricted, cyclical, seasonal migration structured more to variations in elevation and resources *within* the region (Bass 1977; Purrington 1983). Seasonally variable wild foods were obtained by planned seasonal moves to base camps in proximity to diverse resources. Pigweed, goosefoot, sunflower, squash, and bottle gourd were cultivated at spring and summer base camps. Activities at late summer/fall-season base camps were concentrated on gathering and processing mast (acorns, beech nuts, chestnuts, hickory nuts, walnuts) and, undoubtedly, hunting the fauna which also were attracted to the recently fallen mast. Establishment of garden areas and non-portable technology (grinding tools and soapstone vessels) at ideally situated base camps guaranteed repetition of site occupation by one group of people in their cyclical migration within the region.

At prescribed times and locations within the annual cycle, individual groups would have ensured their access to other necessary but heterogeneously distributed resources such as soapstone, quartzite, and rhyolite. This access may have been obtained through direct acquisition, if the resource occurred within the group's territory, through exchange at larger group aggregation encampments, or through exchange with unrelated groups in adjacent or distant territories by means of trade partnerships.

Before leaving this summary of the Late Archaic it is perhaps opportune to discuss linguistic (glottochronological) research, which estimates the divergence of the Cherokee from other Iroquoian language speakers. Cherokee is a language belonging to the Iroquois language family. Floyd G. Lounsbury, a linguistic anthropologist formerly at Yale University, based upon differences between Cherokee and Northern Iroquoian languages, estimated the linguistic divergence from a common ancestral language to have occurred sometime just after 2,000 BCE, in the Late Archaic period (Lounsbury 1961).

The ancestral speakers, among whom this divergence took place, may have resided in the Appalachians, the ultimate home of the Cherokees and various northern Iroquois speakers (Whyte 2007a). Material-cultural links between the northern and southern Appalachian regions include Brewerton and Lamoka-like projectile points of the Late Archaic period, small, stemmed projectile points (Swannanoa and Rossville types) and cord or fabric-marked pottery (Swannanoa and Vinette I types) of the succeeding Early Woodland period. At the same time, cremation appears to have been preferred mode of disposal of the dead throughout the Appalachians. The region is also characterized by a relatively homogeneous mast-forest adaptation. Thus, an Appalachian-specific, mast forest adaptation of hunter-gatherers appears to have been in place by 2,000 BCE. The resident cultures

4. Late Archaic Period: 3,000–1,000 BCE

participated in a network involving alliances and exchange within and beyond the mountains. It was perhaps out of this adaptation that the ancestors of the historic Cherokee and Northern Iroquois emerged. If the glottochronologic estimate of the Cherokee-Iroquois split is reasonably accurate, and if the ancestral stock resided in the Appalachians, the ancestor, but not exclusively, is represented in the archaeological record by Brewerton and Lamoka points, soapstone vessels, cremation burials, and intensive subsistence emphasis on mast and other resources of the chestnut forests that spanned the Appalachian region. That ancestral stock may have consisted of several related and allied tribes which spanned the entire Appalachian chain and controlled and sometimes distributed, by trade and otherwise, its lithic and food resources. Perhaps Iroquois ancestors had resided in the Appalachian Region well before the Late Archaic period or had moved into the region during the Late Archaic period to take advantage of and control its economic riches. Soapstone may have become integral to their ethnic identity, as were ceramics to their contemporaries in the adjacent lowlands (see Sassaman 2001). It is possible that intraregional intertribal conflict over these Appalachian resources, competition from outside, or simply a shift from soapstone technology and mast forest adaptation to the ceramic and horticulture brought on the ultimate dividing and gradual distancing of Cherokee ancestors from the rest of Iroquoia. This may have happened at about 1,700 BCE as estimated by linguistic distance. Or, perhaps the divergence coincided with the breakup of the Appalachian adaptation just a little later. Nevertheless, the speakers of the mother tongue went on their own evolutionary paths to become the Cherokee of the Southern Appalachians and the Northern Iroquois of Laurentia.

5

Early Woodland Period: 1,000 BCE–200 CE

The group arrived early in the evening with two pack dogs, their hunting/foraging gear, dried venison, four loaves of nut bread, a bag of sunflower seeds, a bladder of passenger pigeon oil, and a turkey, gray fox, and a box turtle shell procured while en route to the site. The women set up camp, started a fire, and began boiling water. Before using the fire for cooking, a woman offered the requisite seven sunflower seeds to the fire. The fox and turkey were skinned, gutted, roasted on coals, and then shared and eaten. The carcasses were then boiled for broth and the remaining bones deposited on the ground down-wind of the fire.

The camp is situated in a clearing at the confluence of a large creek and small river where aquatic, terrestrial, and avian food sources are abundant. They will stay here for ten days before descending to lower elevations and warmer climes for the coming winter.

The children made a brush net of tree branches in preparation for fishing the next day. After dark, women took torches and sticks to go "bird brushing" in the thickets near the site. They returned less than an hour later with nine songbirds for roasting. These they placed on embers, carefully turning them for even cooking, until the feathers and feet were burned away. When they were deemed edible, the birds were shared among the group as an evening snack. They were eaten in their entirety, viscera, bones, meat, and all.

Children baited wooden skewers with fox meat and, with the aid of a torch, fished for crayfish in the creek. The ones they captured were placed on coals in the fire and rotated until cooked orange. The meat was relished and the exoskeletons were tossed into the fire.

At daybreak the men left camp to go hunting with bow-and-arrow and blowguns. The women and children went off into the woods to forage for plant foods and small animals. All consumed dried deer meat and chestnut bread that they had brought with them, as well as various

5. Early Woodland Period: 1,000–200 CE

raw nuts, berries, flowers, mushrooms, and seeds encountered along the way. Women and children returned early afternoon with sundry roots, leaves, berries, mushrooms, bags of acorns, hickory nuts, chestnuts, and a rattlesnake. After removing the husks, hickory nuts were mashed using a river cobble on a flat rock. The fragments were gathered and boiled in a large ceramic vessel of water to extract oils. The nutshell fragments were skimmed off and tossed on the ground. Red and white oak acorns were cracked and the nutmeat mashed, using the same tools, to create dough that was formed into small loaves and baked in the ashes of the fire. The nutshells and hickory nut husks were tossed in the fire for fuel.

The children then dragged the brush-net through the creek, collecting a small rock bass, three small brook trout, and a river chub, which, along with the rattlesnake, were added to the pot of hickory nut oil. Using the turtle shell, members of the group took and consumed from the pot when they were hungry. The stew was gradually consumed, and on the morning of their departure the dregs dumped on the ground downwind of the fire.

The men returned to camp at dark with the entire carcass of a white-tailed deer, an eastern gray squirrel, and another wild turkey. The turkey was skinned, gutted, and roasted on the coals. The squirrel was roasted whole on the coals. After the turkey meat was eaten, its carcass was boiled for broth. The deer was gutted, skinned, and filleted into strips of meat for drying on a rack over the fire. The liver and tongue were roasted and consumed. Leg bones were broken open with a stone hammer and anvil to remove the marrow, which was eaten raw. Four elongated splinters of the metatarsi were conserved for tool supply. The remaining bones were tossed on the ground downwind of the fire for the dogs to enjoy. The doe's skull and jaw were placed in the crook of a tree across the creek, facing the forest, so that her spirit could find its way home.

On the tenth day the group left the site by mid-morning, taking with them the dried venison, remaining dried fruits, mushrooms, and berries. Before leaving they ritually smashed the box turtle carapace bowl and tossed the fragments into the smoldering ashes of the campfire. Crows squawking in the overhanging trees anxiously awaited the group's departure. The site was littered with greasy bones and viscera.

******

The primary differences between the preceding Late Archaic period and the Early Woodland period in the Appalachian Summit are the widespread adoption of ceramic technology, a gradual decrease in the use of soapstone, and abandonment of the large stone knives. Other characteristics of the preceding period, such as a decrease in mobility and an increase in social complexity, warfare, and consumption of domesticated weedy annuals only intensified. In the higher elevations of the northwestern counties of North Carolina, Early Woodland period sites consist of small seasonally occupied camps located primarily on river and creek valley margins, saddles and gaps, in rockshelters, and on toe slopes adjacent to springheads. There seems to be less evidence of humans in the Early Woodland period in our part of the Appalachian Summit than in the preceding Late Archaic. This may indicate more prolonged settlement at lower elevations where gardening was more fruitful.

Only one phase, Swannanoa, is typically recognized for the Early Woodland period of the North Carolina Mountains. Named for the Swannanoa River that joins the French Broad River in Asheville, this phase is identified primarily on the basis of the earliest pottery found in the region. Other kinds of pottery dating to the same time period, however, are found in small amounts. These include Long Branch, a limestone-tempered, fabric-marked pottery, and Watts Bar, a quartzite- or sand-tempered, cord- or fabric-marked pottery. Both are found in greater frequency to the west in the VRP.

Addition of fired clay pottery to the cooking and storage technologies of humans in the region undoubtedly had profound impacts on their livelihoods. Materials for making ceramic vessels can be found almost anywhere—they are easily constructed and easily replaced when broken. They also are much more portable than soapstone vessels and, unlike basketry and wooden vessels, they are relatively waterproof and can be placed in and over fires for cooking. They also, being constructed of a plastic medium, provide additional means for artistic and symbolic expression.

Artifacts of the Early Woodland Period

Swannanoa phase pottery, defined on the basis of evidence from the Warren Wilson site in Buncombe County, North Carolina, is described by Keel (1976) as consisting primarily of coil-constructed conoidal jars with coarse sand and crushed quartz tempering (materials mixed with the clay to ensure strength and reduce shrinkage) and cord or fabric marked exteriors (Figure 5.1). Minor surface treatments

5. Early Woodland Period: 1,000–200 CE

Figure 5.1. Early Woodland Swannanoa cord-marked pottery from Church Rockshelter No. 2.

include plain, simple-stamped, and (later) check-stamped. Keel considers this combination of attributes as having a northern origin. Marking the exteriors, using cord or fabric-wrapped paddles or carved wooden stamps helped to weld coils together, imparted textures and symbolism, and increased the surface areas of vessels for more rapid heating.

Watts Bar pottery, defined on the basis of evidence from sites in eastern Tennessee (Lewis and Kneberg 1957), is virtually identical to Swannanoa pottery, the primary difference being the use of crushed quartzite or sand as a tempering agent. Whyte (2018a) considers the two to be one and the same.

Projectile points of this period include several named types, including Swannanoa (Figure 5.2) (Keel 1976) and Ebenezer stemmed forms

Figure 5.2. Early Woodland Swannanoa arrow points from the Katie Griffith site, Watauga County, North Carolina.

Figure 5.3. Early Woodland Ebenezer arrow points.

5. Early Woodland Period: 1,000–200 CE

(Figure 5.3) (Kneberg 1956), Greenville/Camp Creek, and Candy Creek triangular forms (Figure 5.4) (Lewis and Kneberg 1957), Nolichucky Side Notched (Figure 5.5) (Lewis and Kneberg 1957), and Yadkin triangular (Coe 1964), the specific temporal relationships of which remain to be sorted out. However, the stemmed forms appear to largely predate the triangular and side-notched ones. These are arguably arrow points; several Greenville/Camp Creek points were found embedded in bones or within the chest cavities of humans interred at the Camp Creek site in eastern Tennessee, and part of an arrow shaft was found in the deepest level of the site (see below). Camp Creek triangular arrow points are probably smaller versions of Greenville points and therefore typologically invalid.

Other items found on Early Woodland sites include the usual array

— 1 cm

Figure 5.4. Early Woodland Greenville/Camp Creek (top) and Candy Creek (bottom) arrow points.

Figure 5.5. Early Woodland Nolichucky arrow points from Church Rockshelter No. 2, Watauga County, North Carolina.

of cobble tools (grinding stones, hammer stones), scrapers, drills, and flake tools, and bone and antler tools. Soapstone vessels continue in use through much of the period, eventually giving way to ceramic cooking vessels. Other ground stone objects include tubular medicine pipes of soft stone, "birdstones," and two-holed gorgets possibly representing symbols or ornaments (Figure 5.6). Birdstones and gorgets are rarely found on small upland campsites; their functions remain a mystery.

5. Early Woodland Period: 1,000–200 CE

Figure 5.6. Early Woodland birdstone (a), gorget (b), and pipe (c).

Mountain Life in the Early Woodland Period

There is little change in the uplands from earlier Archaic times other than the introduction of ceramics and the discontinued use of the large stone knives and ultimately, soapstone vessels. Here, people appear to have remained hunters and gatherers of wild foods with a horticultural (pepo squash, gourd, sunflower, maygrass, knotweed, pigweed, marsh elder) supplement. Maize may have been introduced to the Southeast in the Early Woodland period but does not appear to have become a measurable part of the diet until much later. Evidence from the Camp Creek site (see below) indicates a broad-based hunting and gathering food economy but with an emphasis on white-tailed deer.

Sites such as Warren Wilson near Asheville, and Camp Creek in the VRP of eastern Tennessee, show evidence of long-term and repeated use but may still have been seasonally abandoned. Early Woodland sites in the uplands of northwestern North Carolina consist of small campsites located on the terraces and alluvial fans of rivers and streams, in rockshelters, and at the heads of springs and in mountain gaps and saddles. These sites typically contain a smattering of pottery sherds, arrow points and other chipped stone tools, and concentrations of burned rocks. Food remains from this period in the mountains are all but absent unless preserved in rockshelter settings. Again, much of what we know about human life in this period must be derived from neighboring sites in the foothills where preservation is better and where mountain visitors may have resided during much of the year.

In earlier periods it is to some extent possible to determine the general directions from which these migrants came based upon the geologic sources of the lithic materials of which their stone tools were made. This is problematic in the Early Woodland period, however, because many of their tools were made from earlier artifacts that they had found discarded by previous migrants to the area (Whyte 2014). It was noted (Whyte 2003) that Early Woodland pottery recovered from the Katie Griffith site in northern Watauga County contained none of the small black biotite particles typical of locally made pottery of later times. This indicates that this pottery was made elsewhere and brought to the site by Early Woodland migrants seasonally visiting the uplands (Whyte 2003). Such seasonal visits, again, would have been most beneficial in late summer and fall. Small groups or individual families may have come to the area from lower elevations east and west, bringing their pottery and other utensils and tools needed for harvesting and processing abundant seasonal food resources.

These migratory groups seasonally visiting the uplands of northwestern North Carolina may have splintered off from larger groups of villagers residing in the lowlands to the east and west. Those villages, such as the Camp Creek site, because of their size and the evidence of warfare may have had a loose form of leadership, perhaps in the form of a "big man" whose status was achieved rather than ascribed. They also may have had a slightly more complicated tribal social structure in which clan and age groups had special status or recognition. Anthropologists call these societies "transegalitarian" because they are intermediate between egalitarian societies and those ruled by a chief. However, there is no evidence of preferential treatment of the dead, an indication of social status differentiation, among the many human burials at the Camp Creek site. It was perhaps only later that an individual's status in life was extended to the afterlife.

Church Rockshelter No. 2, Watauga County, North Carolina

A small recess in the cliff face overlooking Watauga River below its confluence with Dutch Creek, near Valle Crucis, North Carolina, was excavated by artifact collectors in the early 1970s and then by ASU

5. Early Woodland Period: 1,000–200 CE

archaeologists in 1975 and 2011 (Whyte 2013c). Church Rockshelter No. 2 (CR2) includes two small areas of soil accumulation. The lower, larger area had been thoroughly excavated by artifact collectors and in 1975 by ASU archaeologists. The smaller, more elevated space to the south appeared to be undisturbed prior to the 2011 excavations. Two adjacent 1 × 1 m units excavated in this space yielded artifacts dating primarily to the Early Woodland period. These include 33 sherds of a single conoidal ceramic vessel that was cord marked and tempered with finely crushed quartz, biotite, and muscovite (Figure 5.1). This temper likely was produced by crushing a weathered piece of muscovite biotite schist. The sherds were recovered from approximately 53 cm below surface. Because of this combination of tempering materials, Whyte (2013c) referred to this pottery as Watts Bar. Two of these sherds were dated by means of optically stimulated luminescence (OSL) to approximately 1,080 BCE (Whyte 2018a).

Fire cracked and reddened rocks were surprisingly few and included more from alluvial sources (the nearby river) than colluvial material that had broken away from the shelter face. The latter may represent inadvertent exposure to fire while the former may have been carefully selected for hot-rock boiling and other warming/cooking processes. Cobble tools include hammer and anvil stones recovered from the lower shelter area.

Chipped stone debitage, recovered primarily from the lower shelter area, include a combination of byproducts of bifacial thinning (soft-hammer percussion), core reduction (primarily hard-hammer percussion), and bipolar (compression) flaking. These include both flakes and cores of various local (quartz) and non-local materials. The latter primarily derive from VRP formations some 30 kilometers to the west and include Knox chert, Shady chalcedony, Del Rio jasper, and Erwin quartzite. A few artifacts of Mount Rogers formation rhyolite from 48 kilometers to the northeast, and Uwharrie formation dacite from 193 kilometers or more to the east were also recovered.

Temporally diagnostic knives and projectile points recovered span the Middle Archaic through Late Woodland periods. Most of these were recovered from the more commodious lower shelter area. Included are Middle Archaic Morrow Mountain types, Late/Terminal Archaic Lamoka, Iddins, and Appalachian Stemmed types, Early Woodland (Nolichucky) types, Late Woodland triangular types, and Late Woodland/Mississippian Jack's Reef and Pisgah serrated points. Early Woodland period projectile points are especially numerous. The absence of vertical patterning with typological age indicates extreme disturbance to the deposits in the lower shelter area. It is also possible, if not likely, that all of the Archaic period tools had been found elsewhere, reused, and deposited by later Woodland period visitors to the site (Whyte 2014).

Fragments of animal bone, teeth, and shells were recovered by each of the excavations. These include bones of amphibians, reptiles, birds, and mammals that may represent human food or the deposits of nonhuman carnivorous denizens. Specifically identifiable bone specimens include a trunk vertebra of a hellbender, two vertebrae of a toad, an eastern box turtle carapace fragment, a proximal phalanx of a wild turkey, a distal metatarsal of a rabbit, and nine specimens identified as white-tailed deer. The latter include all portions of the anatomy. Most of the specimens preserved on the site had been calcined or charred. None shows evidence of artificial modification. Only the burnt specimens can be considered as anthropogenic with any degree of certainty.

The Early Woodland component of the site is indicated by Nolichucky type arrow points and Watts Bar cord-marked and plain-surfaced pottery. While Purrington (1975; 1983) assigned all small shallow-side-notched projectile points to the Middle Woodland Pigeon type defined by Keel (1976), they are not associated with Pigeon ceramics in this part of the state, and the examples recovered from CR2 are morphologically indistinguishable from Nolichucky points recovered from the Camp Creek site (Lewis and Kneberg 1957) located 50 kilometers to the southwest and defined by Kneberg (1957). All but two (one chalcedony and one Uwharrie rhyolite) are made of Erwin formation quartzite, the nearest geologic source of which is approximately 24 kilometers downstream and to the west. That most of these are rose colored, whereas the natural color of the iron-rich material is light beige or yellow, suggests the possibility that they or the parent materials from which they were made were intentionally thermally altered, presumably to impart color change. The one made of Uwharrie dacite, the geologic source of which is found well east of the distribution of the point type, was likely fashioned from an earlier artifact that had been found and recycled (see Whyte 2014). The morphologies of these points and the discovery of a carbonized arrow shaft stratigraphically beneath them at the Camp Creek site (Lewis and Kneberg 1957) suggest that they are arrow points.

Considering the degree of contextual disturbance in the lower shelter area where all but one of the Nolichucky points were found,

5. Early Woodland Period: 1,000–200 CE

it is impossible to confirm a ceramic type association for them at this site. However, a likely association is the Watts Bar cord-marked and plain-surfaced pottery found in both parts of the shelter. This association is well established at Camp Creek (Lewis and Kneberg 1957) and sites of the Phipps Bend project (Lafferty 1981), both in northeastern Tennessee. The Watts Bar pottery at this site was probably locally made or made where clays and sands could be derived from sources along the Watauga and Nolichucky Rivers that erode the Alligator Back formation.

Inferring the precise reasons for human activity in CR2 on the basis of materials recovered and the physical structure of the site is problematic. Use of the term "shelter" in defining the site carelessly assumes that the site functioned as a temporary place for human habitation, perhaps during inclement weather, and that all of the accumulated materials represent the suite of activities expected for a temporary seasonal residence. Indeed, all of the animal and plant remains, stone tools, stone debitage, and ceramic artifacts recovered can accommodate a temporary residence scenario that is typically used to explain most evidence found in rockshelters of the region. However, recent studies by Claassen and Compton (2012) and Whyte (2005; 2007b; 2018b) have introduced the possibility that rockshelters of the region were regarded much like caves and frequently hosted ritual activities such as human burial and offerings to spirits. Many of artifacts recovered from CR2, and especially the pottery, may represent offerings. Broken projectile points, unmodified flakes, and small bifacial tool retouch flakes in the deposits evince weaponry maintenance. In all probability the site was used for both profane and sacred purposes.

The Camp Creek Site

Although it is located somewhat to the west of the Appalachian Summit along the Nolichucky River in the VRP of eastern Tennessee, the Camp Creek site, excavated by the Tennessee Archaeological Society in the mid–1950s, is worth discussing here because of its remarkable organic preservation and the fact that its residents may have been seasonal visitors to northwestern North Carolina in the Early Woodland period (Lewis and Kneberg 1957). Preservation of organic remains such as human and animal bone and mollusk shell is exceptional because of the calcium-rich soils overlying the weathered limestone bedrock. Contexts were well preserved because periodic flooding of Camp

Boone Before Boone

Creek and the Nolichucky River gently blanketed the site with enough sediment to seal and protect the deeper archaeological remains from historic cultivation and other surface disturbances.

Because stratigraphic distinctions were indiscernible, the site was excavated in six arbitrary one-foot levels to subsoil. Several features, including hearths, food storage pits, dog burials, and human burials were encountered and excavated. Only isolated post molds indicated the former existence of some kind of architecture. Animal bones, unless they had been fashioned into tools, implements, or ornaments, were not saved by the excavators. However, bones of deer, elk, bear, wild turkey, and small rodents, as well as shells of mussels and snails (*Io spinosa*) were purportedly found. The tip of a quartzite point was found embedded in an elk scapula. A sample of charcoal recovered from Level C (2–3 feet depth), submitted to the University of Michigan Radiocarbon Laboratory, yielded an estimate of 100 BCE (Lewis and Kneberg 1957).

Chipped stone tools and weaponry recovered include hundreds of projectile points, scrapers, drills, and knives. Most projectile points are of Early Woodland types such as Greenville and Nolichucky. Most of these are made of locally occurring Knox chert and Erwin quartzite. The Greenville points are large triangular arrow points that likely represent some of the earliest residence at the site. The slightly later Nolichucky points are smaller triangular forms with shallow side notches for hafting. Other stone artifacts recovered from the site are cut mica, ground slate gorgets, celts, hoes, hammer stones, anvil stones, ground hematite, steatite and sandstone pipes, and boat stones and bird stones that may have been parts of weaponry.

Most of the approximately 1,500 pottery sherds recovered from the site are assignable to the Early Woodland Long Branch type. This pottery consists of conoidal jars tempered with crushed limestone and marked on the exterior with fabric. This type is uncommon in the higher elevations of the Appalachian Summit, possibly because of the lack of limestone in the region. At the Camp Creek site, it was probably culturally affiliated with the Greenville points recovered. The second most abundant type of pottery is Watts Bar, tempered with sand and/or crushed quartzite and marked on the exterior with fabric or cord. This type of pottery was probably associated with the Nolichucky arrow points at the site.

Modified marine shell objects include disk-shaped beads and gorgets carved from the whorls of whelk (probably *Sinistrofulgar perversum*) shells, tubular beads carved from whelk shell columellas, and

5. Early Woodland Period: 1,000–200 CE

beads fashioned from *Olivella* and *Marginalla* shells. Nearly all of these were found with human burials. Modified vertebrate remains include many pointed bone tools carved from deer antlers and turkey and deer leg and foot bones, antler billets (presumed to have served in the flaking of stone), an antler comb, drilled elk canine teeth, drilled bear and raccoon canines, bone fish hooks, turtle carapace containers, ornately carved bone pins, and modified bear and deer jaws. Carbonized plant remains were abundant at the site but only some carbonized wood was saved for radiocarbon dating. Also found in burials were several beads of copper, possibly imported from copper sources in the Midwest.

More than 50 human burials were excavated, including those of children and adult males and females. One mass grave appeared to have contained the remains of a single family that was murdered:

> Four instances of multiple burials were uncovered during the first season, and another including eleven individuals has recently been excavated. One from the first season's work apparently represents the massacre of an entire family. There was an adult male, an adult female, two children and another adult of indeterminate sex. The adult female had a Greenville point lodged in the right side of a neck vertebra; the adult male had a similar Greenville point in the right shoulder blade, and a Camp Creek point in the chest cavity; and one of the children had a Greenville point in the right forearm and a Camp Creek point in the chest cavity [Lewis and Kneberg 1957:32].

Several other burials included evidence of embedded arrow points and other inflicted wounds, suggesting that Early Woodland peoples of the region were actively engaged in interpersonal violence and probably endemic (within the region) warfare. On adult male had suffered many inflicted injuries:

> An old healed fracture or very deep injury on the left frontal bone appears to have been caused by a downward blow with a sharp weapon such as a celt. In the left parietal bone is a more spectacular injury. A hole almost three-quarters of an inch in diameter which was well healed around the edges, represents a depressed skull fracture made with a blunt instrument such as the poll of a Woodland celt.... It is quite obvious that the man survived the injuries for a considerable time, only to meet death later from another attack—that time from arrows. Four projectile points, one unclassifiable, one Nolichucky, one undifferentiated triangular and one Appalachian Stemmed lay in position suggesting that they had been shot into the individual [Lewis and Kneberg 1957:35].

One of the most significant finds at the site was the proximal end of a carbonized cane arrow shaft that had been nocked for insertion of the bowstring (Figure 5.7). This was found at the very base of the excavations, preserved below a cluster of freshwater mussel shell, and

— 1 cm

Figure 5.7. The back end of a carbonized river cane arrow recovered from an Early Woodland stratum at the Camp Creek site, Greene County, Tennessee (courtesy of the Frank H. McClung Museum of Natural History & Culture, University of Tennessee, Knoxville).

represents the earliest conclusive evidence of the use of bow-and-arrow technology in the region. It also indicates that the Greenville/Camp Creek, Candy Creek, and Nolichucky points were on the tips of arrows rather than spears. Although many of the collections from the Camp Creek site were donated by the excavators to the University of Tennessee and are now safe in the Frank H. McClung Museum of Natural History & Culture in Knoxville, the collection that included the arrow shaft was not, and has since been stolen.

The Camp Creek site was clearly a multi-season base camp where its residents, egalitarian hunter-gatherer-horticulturalists, lived, died, and were buried for perhaps decades. The site may have been seasonally abandoned, perhaps in the fall or spring when heavy rains threatened to flood the site. The occupants were engaged in systems of long-distance exchange, as indicated by the presence of marine shell and copper. These items, as well as the steatite platform pipes and modified mammal jaws recovered, indicate some influence by or interaction with Adena peoples of the lower Midwest. They also were regularly engaged in endemic warfare, as evidenced by the many embedded arrow points and other inflicted wounds. That the embedded and associated arrow points are of the same types and materials as those found among the sites refuse deposits indicates conflict with related, neighboring groups.

Summary

The Early Woodland period in the Appalachian Summit and adjacent foothills is best summarized as a period of increasing human population, sedentism, territoriality, and possibly warfare. The archaeological evidence of this is: the presence of large semi-permanent residences such as the Camp Creek and Warren Wilson sites containing many human burials; cultivation of plant foods; items such as marine shell ornaments indicating long-distance exchange; use of relatively

5. Early Woodland Period: 1,000–200 CE

non-portable technology such as large ceramic and soapstone vessels; increased reliance on bow-and-arrow weaponry; and considerable numbers of inflicted wounds among skeletal remains. However, archaeological sites in the higher elevations, such as around Boone, North Carolina, are small seasonal camps and resource extraction sites at which smaller groups resided very temporarily on their way through the uplands or from which they foraged and hunted.

Inhabitants of the Appalachian Summit appear to have been minimally influenced by more complex cultural phenomena brewing in the Ohio and upper Mississippi Valleys between 1,000 and 200 BCE. There, in what is known as Adena Culture, people shared in a ceremonial complex involving construction of earthen mounds, creation of elaborate iconography, and participation in long-distance exchange for the acquisition of marine shell and copper. Adena set the stage for the subsequent and more expansive Hopewell phenomenon of the Middle Woodland period, which did find its way into the Appalachian Summit Region.

6

Middle Woodland Period: 200–900 CE

The villagers, having fasted for seven days, were gathered at sunset on benches around the fire in the musty, dark earth-lodge to celebrate the annual world renewal ceremony. On the outside, the building resembles a squarish earthen mound. It is essentially an artificial cave representing the underground from which humans and all land animals were born and to which their spirits would return upon death. On this night the sun had set behind its most southern point on the horizon. Tomorrow's sunrise would signify the lengthening of days and the return of the sun to its dominion. Yesterday the earth lodge was prepared, first by evicting the village dogs that considered it their den when humans weren't using it, second by clearing out their dung, gnawed deer bones, and other debris, and lastly by igniting the sacred fire and purifying the air with burning red cedar leaves.

Gola, now thirteen years old, sat on a bench along the inner walls with the rest of her village to witness the ceremony through the haze of wood smoke wending its way to the hole in the roof. She was in wonderment that the men were able to erect the big pine tree for the sacred center post of the lodge. They had trimmed its branches, pulled it with ropes over logs from a great distance, charred its base, and hoisted it into the big hole in the ground using ropes and poles. This post connected the lower, middle, and upper worlds of their universe.

A lone drummer began to play the heartbeat of the people and the earth. One by one, painted dancers regaled in feathers and animal skins, and wearing turtle shell rattles on their ankles entered through the small opening into the stifling cavern. They danced and sang, first clockwise around the fire, then counterclockwise. Their rattles evoked the power of the timber rattler, revered as a protector from the sun. In the dark, smoky space and in the flickering firelight, they appeared to Gola as living animal spirits.

6. Middle Woodland Period: 200–900 CE

When the song was over and the drumming ceased, a shape shifter came through the opening, snarling and inspiring great awe with his appearance. He was covered in sewn wolf hides and wore the skin of a wolf's head and face as a hat, and a wolf's rostrum and jaw as a mask. He had become a wolf. The drum was started again, inviting the wolf to begin his quadrupedal dance that would free and guide the sun from its hiding place beneath the earth to its dominion in the sky. Then entered another shape shifter who had become a black bear, shaking his skin and growling to the drumbeat. The bear was a spirit-guide who spent the winter underground and whose emergence in spring would herald the return of the sun and the Earth's bounty. When she was younger and had attended the winter dance Gola trembled in fear of these man-animals. But now, when they danced before her, she was merely awed by their power.

Many sacred songs were sung and dances danced. Tired drummers passed their sticks to their replacements without missing a beat. The drumming stopped only when clan leaders stood to tell the ancient stories of creation and how the animals placed the sun in the sky. One by one, children fell asleep in the laps of their mothers and older siblings. Gola promised herself that this year she would stay awake as did the adults. Nevertheless, because her eyes stung, her lungs begged for oxygen, and she was terribly hungry, the wolf and bear became real, and she fell asleep.

At dawn the people emerged to watch the sunrise from its lowest point on the ridge to the southeast. Then they prepared a great feast of meats, loaves of bread made from acorns, and stew. The remains of the feast and ceremony, including intentionally broken clay vessels, stone blades, bone pins, baskets, and costume, were strewn over and around the earth lodge. To omit this ritual would ensure eternal winter.

******

There is little evidence of humans in the upper Watauga and New River valleys of the Appalachian Summit between 200 and 900 CE. The few small sites containing this evidence, as in previous times, indicate seasonal migration from the Piedmont Plateau to the east and the VRP to the west. At lower elevations, however, such as along the Swannanoa, French Broad, Little Tennessee, and Pigeon rivers to the southwest, there are large residential sites, some with mounds and permanent structures. These differences between the northwestern and southwestern areas of the state may indicate that the latter region was occupied and controlled by a resident population of humans, possibly the ancestors of the Cherokees (Kimball and Wolf 2017), while the former was shared ground seasonally exploited by unrelated groups. This division would remain evident through the remainder of precontact times.

There are several phases of the Middle Woodland period represented in the Appalachian Summit, and these were named for clusters of archaeological traits (pottery, arrow points, etc.) identified on some of the first sites of the period that were investigated. For example, Patricia Holden (1966) first described the Pigeon and Connestee phases based on surface collections from her archaeological surveys in Transylvania County, North Carolina. The Pigeon phase probably lasted from about 200–300 CE. Radiocarbon dates from Garden Creek Mound No. 2 in Haywood County, North Carolina, indicated initial mound construction in the late Pigeon phase (Wright 2020). The subsequent Connestee phase dates to between 300 and 800 CE. Bennie Keel (1976) further elucidated the Pigeon and Connestee phases based on evidence from the excavations by the University of North Carolina at the Garden Creek site in Haywood County and Warren Wilson site in Buncombe County.

The Candy Creek phase is coeval with Connestee and is recognized by a very similar ceramic industry—pottery tempered with crushed limestone and marked on the exterior with cord impressions (Kneberg 1961). This pottery is found mostly on the western fringe of the Appalachian Summit in eastern Tennessee. The primary difference between Connestee and Candy Creek is the tempering material and the geographic distributions of the types, although both types were found in features and other contexts at the Icehouse Bottom site in eastern Tennessee (Chapman and Keel 1979).

Another kind of Middle Woodland pottery, more common in the northwestern counties of the state, is also limestone tempered but impressed on the exterior with a finely woven looped net. Vessel interiors are heavily scraped. Charcoal in a feature that contained this pottery was radiocarbon dated to about 670 CE (Riggs 1985). Because it is limestone tempered, net impressed, and scraped on the interior this may be a very early form of the Radford series, primarily a Late Woodland period pottery common in southwestern Virginia (Evans 1955). This kind of pottery is often found in rockshelters along the Watauga River in North Carolina, evidently deposited by migratory groups entering the uplands from the VRP downriver.

6. Middle Woodland Period: 200–900 CE

Artifacts of the Middle Woodland Period

Most of the Middle Woodland period pottery found in rockshelters and on small open-air sites along the Watauga and New Rivers is assignable to three of the phases mentioned above: Connestee, Candy Creek, and the unnamed limestone tempered pottery found in the Watauga River valley of eastern Tennessee (Riggs 1985). Purrington (1983) labeled many sites in the northwestern mountains "Pigeon phase sites" based primarily on the finding of small side-notched arrow points that resemble ones found with Pigeon pottery at the Warren Wilson site. However, very little Pigeon pottery has been found in the northwestern counties and a reanalysis of these arrow points (Whyte 2013c) indicates that they are actually earlier Nolichucky points. Pigeon phase pottery, more abundant in the southwestern part of the state, is a thin-walled, crushed quartz–tempered ware that was primarily check-stamped on the exterior with a carved paddle (Figure 6.1). The interiors of sherds have a distinctive

Figure 6.1. Middle Woodland Pigeon check-stamped pottery from the Warren Wilson site, Buncombe County, North Carolina (courtesy of the Research Laboratories of Archaeology, University of North Carolina at Chapel Hill).

Figure 6.2. Middle Woodland Connestee cord-marked pottery from the Biltmore Mound site, Buncombe County, North Carolina.

sheen that may have been imparted by rubbing the leather-hard clay with a soapstone pebble (Keel 1976). Vessel forms include bowls, conoidal jars, and jars with flat bottoms and large tetrapodal supports.

Connestee pottery, named for the mythical Cherokee town of Kanasta, is tempered with sand and plain, brushed, simple stamped, or cord marked on the exterior (Figure 6.2). The thin-walled vessels include conical and hemispherical shapes. Some large storage vessels have flat bases with tetrapodal supports. Other artifacts associated with the Connestee phase are medium-sized triangular arrow points with straight to excurvate blades. In the northwestern counties, these are often made of Del Rio yellow and red jasper originating in eastern Tennessee (Figure 6.3). Other artifacts of this phase are small blades and blade cores of flint, clay pipes, slate gorgets, clay figurines, and symbolic items made from sheet mica. At mound and village sites such as Garden Creek in Haywood County and Biltmore in Asheville, exotic artifacts have been found that include microblades made of Flint Ridge chalcedony, a colorful flint-like material from central Ohio, and items of copper and pieces of Chillicothe Rocker-stamped pottery, also imported from the Midwest (Keel 1976; Kimball et al. 2010). In exchange, large sheets of mica, chipped stone objects made from crystal quartz, chlorite schist for making pipes and ornaments, and perhaps black bear hides, claws, and teeth were exported from the Appalachian Summit. The microblades had various functions, including meat cutting, mica cutting, and woodworking (Kimball and Wolf 2017). Mica cutouts of a human hand and a hawk's talons made from Appalachian region mica were found at

6. Middle Woodland Period: 200–900 CE

——— 1 cm

Figure 6.3. Middle Woodland Connestee triangular arrow points.

the Hopewell Mound Group in Ross County, Ohio. This evidence indicates participation of Appalachian Summit residents in the "Hopewell Interaction Sphere" named for its links to the Hopewell Mound group in Ohio, and which had its roots in the Adena phenomenon of the same region (Caldwell 1964).

Candy Creek pottery is tempered with finely crushed limestone and mostly cord marked, but sometimes plain or simple stamped. It was found with Connestee pottery at the Icehouse Bottom site in eastern Tennessee and appears to be coeval (Chapman and Keel 1979). Very few Candy Creek sherds have been found in the northwestern counties of North Carolina. A few were recovered from the Wakeman III site at an elevation of 4,000 feet near Zionville in Watauga County (Figure 6.4) (Purrington 1983).

——— 1 cm

Figure 6.4. Middle Woodland Candy Creek cord-marked pottery from the Wakeman III site, Watauga County, North Carolina.

Boone Before Boone

Mountain Life in the Middle Woodland Period

Connestee phase sites include villages/hamlets with mounds, village/hamlets lacking mounds, and temporary campsites on various landforms and special purpose sites in rockshelters. Three of the better-known sites are Garden Creek on the Pigeon River in Haywood County, North Carolina, Biltmore Mound on the Biltmore Estate in Asheville, North Carolina, and Icehouse Bottom in Monroe County, Tennessee. These sites are located along major Native American trade paths, and with immediate access to high quality mica and crystal quartz (Biltmore and Garden Creek) or Knox chert (Icehouse Bottom) that was exported to the Midwest and elsewhere. The Middle Woodland mounds at Garden Creek and Biltmore are composed of layers of deliberately selected soil layers of different colors and textures and gathered from different sources hypothesized to represent the recreation of the world (Kimball et al. 2010). Structures on the mounds were sometimes dismantled after use by pulling posts out of the ground and filling in the post holes with river sands or pebbles (Keel 1976; Kimball et al. 2010; Wright 2019). Biltmore mound included what may be the remains of an earth-covered lodge that hosted world-renewal or solstice celebrations and rituals (Figure 6.5) (Kimball and Wolf 2017). Another site with possible evidence of Connestee solstice ritual is Wiseman's View rockshelter

Figure 6.5. Artist's reconstruction of the Biltmore Mound earth lodge (3-D rendering by John Wolf).

6. Middle Woodland Period: 200–900 CE

Figure 6.6. Summer Solstice sunrise (left) and Winter Solstice sunrise (right) as viewed from Wiseman's View, Burke County, North Carolina.

in the Linville Gorge of Burke County, North Carolina (Whyte 2018b). In the 1960s fragments of a single Connestee cord-marked vessel were found in a small rocky alcove of the cliff face below Wiseman's View Overlook. When summer solstice sunrise is viewed from this vantage, the sun rises from behind Hawksbill Mountain on a declination of 60°. When winter solstice sunrise is viewed from this point, the sun rises from behind Table Rock Mountain on a declination of 120° (Figure 6.6) (Whyte 2018b). The vessel and possibly its long-perished contents may have been an offering to the sun. Many people claim to have seen the legendary Brown Mountain Lights from this same place (Clark 1993).

Until recently, little was known of Middle Woodland period domestic architecture in the Appalachian Summit. A study of Early-Middle Woodland architecture to the west in Kentucky (Applegate 2013) indicates a predominance of circular or oval domestic architecture. However, Wright's (2013) recent study of post holes of the pre-mound village at the Garden Creek site reveals probable domestic structures that were squarish, measuring between three and five meters on a side, and roughly squared with the cardinal directions. These post-in-ground structures had straight walls and possibly pyramidal roofs. This shift to rectangular architecture in the Middle Woodland period may symbolize something about the social structure of Middle Woodland societies. Circular domestic architecture is most often associated with egalitarian societies, in which all households have equal status and access to resources. Rectangular domestic architecture is most often found among non-egalitarian societies such as chiefdoms and states, in which status and access to resources are disparate among households and individuals.

No evidence of permanent villages in the Middle Woodland period has been found in the northwestern counties of North Carolina. Use of the higher uplands seems to have remained unchanged. Small groups visiting the area seasonally to obtain their needs left behind only small campsites littered with stone artifacts and a few pottery sherds. Some visitors appear to have come from the VRP to the west, following the Watauga River, bringing artifacts of chert, jasper, and chalcedony, and limestone tempered pottery. Others may have come from the south-southwest where Connestee pottery is concentrated and larger residential sites are found.

Subsistence remains recovered from Garden Creek and Biltmore were found almost exclusively in association with the mounds. In all probability these represent the remains of ritual feasts and therefore may provide a skewed picture of the overall Middle Woodland diet (Kimball et al. 2010; Whyte 2011). Remains of plant and animal foods were especially well preserved at Biltmore (see below) and indicated a focus on white-tailed deer, turkey, squirrel, and box turtle for meat, although remains of freshwater mussels, crayfish, amphibians, fishes, snakes, and a variety of birds and mammals were identified among the tens of thousands of specimens. Plant foods identified include hickory nuts, chestnuts, and acorns as well as goosefoot, knotweed, maygrass, little barley, and sumpweed. Only sparse evidence of maize cultivation or consumption has yet been found on Middle Woodland sites in the Appalachian Summit. The earliest directly dated maize specimen in the region (465±70 CE) was recovered from a Connestee phase context at the California Creek site, 30 km north of Biltmore Mound in Madison County (Crites 1998).

Considering the evidence of villages, rectangular structures, mounds, communal rituals, and long-distance exchange or extra-regional social interaction at sites such as Garden Creek and Biltmore, Middle Woodland groups had probably achieved a more complex transegalitarian social structure in which certain individuals enjoyed a status that afforded them more control over community-wide events such as mound building, ceremonies, and possibly warfare, as well as production and exchange of commodities. These individuals may have been what anthropologists call "big men" who acquired their status through successful economic negotiations.

Little is known of the ways in which Middle Woodland peoples of the Appalachian Summit disposed of their dead. No burials or cremains of this period were encountered in excavations of Garden Creek Mound No. 2 or at Biltmore. At the Macon County Industrial Park, a Connestee phase site in southwestern North Carolina, one burial was found in which the individual lay extended and supine with his head resting on a sheet of mica. Another adjacent grave included the skeletal remains of four individuals crowded together in a single grave. Collins (1977) interprets this as evidence of some degree of status differentiation in Connestee society.

Biltmore Mound, Asheville, North Carolina

On the Biltmore Estate in Asheville, North Carolina, along the Swannanoa River just above its confluence with the French Broad, lie the remains of Biltmore Mound, constructed between 400 and 600 CE (Kimball et al. 2010). Appalachian State University archaeologists excavated the southwestern quarter of the mound in four seasons of work between 2000 and 2008 (Figure 6.7). Historic plowing had reduced the mound to only its lowest layers of construction, but several mound layers, post holes, features, and the surrounding ditch remained in evidence to determine something of its original form and contents. The mound was originally square with rounded corners and approximately 30 meters wide by 2 meters high. It was initially constructed of variable colors and textures of soil, including layers of dark brown, light brown, reddish, and greenish-gray soils gathered from a variety of sources. Surrounding the mound was a ditch that had been carefully lined with a variety of sediments and then filled with three layers of midden containing extraordinary amounts of artifacts, and plant and animal remains. Posts were then erected in the center of the ditch in a line surrounding the mound.

At the center of the mound a large pole (tree trunk) measuring 50 cm in diameter was erected in a deep hole with the aid of an insertion ramp and probably levers and ropes. This pole may represent an "axis mundi" symbolizing a connection between the lower, middle and upper worlds of the cosmos as perceived by many historically documented Native American groups in the Southeast (Kelly 2003:124; Kimball and Wolf 2017). The earth lodge or "great house" situated on the mound was approximately 24 meters wide and constructed with up to 48 outer wall posts and several posts on the interior to support the earth-covered roof

Figure 6.7. Excavation of Biltmore Mound, Buncombe County, North Carolina.

(Kimball and Wolf 2017). It undoubtedly had a central sacred hearth, which remains to be discovered immediately northeast of ASU's excavation block.

Artifacts recovered from Biltmore Mound, especially numerous in its surrounding ditch feature, include thousands of Connestee pottery sherds, thousands of pieces of burned river cobbles (presumably remains of cooking facilities), thousands of chipped stone artifacts such as flakes, cores, microblades, and arrow points, fragments of mica, copper, and marine shell objects, pieces of slate gorgets and clay pipes, and ground pigment minerals. In addition, tens of thousands of plant and animal specimens were recovered. Animal parts fashioned into artifacts include modified canid (wolf and dog) and bear mandibles and rostra (Figure 6.8), pointed bone objects made primarily from deer metatarsi and antler tines (Figure 6.9), and modified box turtle shells, nearly all of which appear to have been ritually broken, and some of which may have been ritually burned, to free the objects' spirits. These were undoubtedly items involved in rituals associated with the mound.

6. Middle Woodland Period: 200–900 CE

Figure 6.8. Modified wolf (a & b) and dog (c) mandibles from Biltmore Mound, Buncombe County, North Carolina.

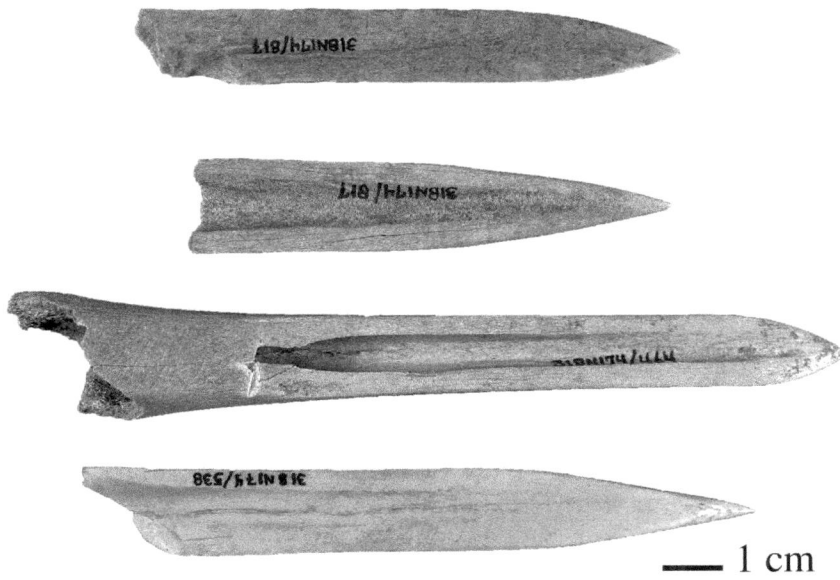

Figure 6.9. Pointed bone implements from Biltmore Mound, Buncombe County, North Carolina.

Construction of the mound itself was a ritualized communal process necessitating the gathering of soils with color and source symbolism, possibly associated with world renewal. The structure on top of the mound housed community ritual events, some of which appear to have been associated with solstice events (Kimball and Wolf 2017). Much of the animal bone recovered from the mound shows evidence of carnivore gnawing and digestion, probably resulting from village dogs availing themselves of the remains of feasts associated with the mound. When it was not in use by the humans, dogs may have used the earth lodge as a place of protection from the heat, cold, wind, rain, and snow.

Animal remains recovered from the site include those of many species of fishes, amphibians, reptiles, birds and mammals, as well as shells of freshwater mussels and exoskeletal parts of crayfish, indicating a diverse diet for the site occupants and a wide variety of foods associated with ritual feasting centered on the mound. The unusual degree of preservation of animal remains at Biltmore (indicated by recovery of whole fish scales, turkey egg shell fragments, and crayfish parts) is probably due to the fact that so many of them were concentrated together, essentially overpowering the effects of soil acidity on calcium dissolution. Remains of white-tailed deer, black bear, wild turkey, and eastern box turtles are particularly abundant. The Biltmore faunal assemblage composition, with its emphasis on white-tailed deer, box turtles, turkeys, and a variety of small mammals fits the expected pattern of feasting provisioned by and involving local community members, but possibly entertaining visiting Hopewellian dignitaries. Deer skeletal part representation is cosmopolitan and bone fragmentation is relatively high, suggesting a low sociopolitical scaling. This feasting may have happened at various times of the year; the abundance of remains of cold-blooded animals and turkey egg shell indicates summer, while deer age estimates indicate fall (Kimball et al. 2010).

The Middle Woodland period residents of the Biltmore site were connected with Hopewell societies in the Ohio valley over 300 kilometers to the Northwest. Objects found on the site originating from the Midwest include pottery, blades of Flint Ridge chalcedony, copper beads, and possibly a gray wolf jaw. Objects of marine shell link them also with traders connected to the Gulf or South Atlantic coasts. In exchange, sheets of mica or objects cut from them, and possibly black bear parts and other materials common in the Appalachian Summit were exported. Another connection with societies in the Hopewell heartland is the sharing of beliefs involving ritualized landscapes and cosmology.

The Garden Creek Site Complex

The Garden site complex is a combination of three Middle Woodland period (about 100–390 CE) mounds, two enclosures, and a village,

6. Middle Woodland Period: 200–900 CE

along with a later Mississippian (1290–1420 CE) mound (Garden Creek Mound No. 1) overlooking the Pigeon River in Haywood County, North Carolina. Salvage excavations of Mound No. 2 were first undertaken by UNC–Chapel Hill in the 1960s due to threats to the site by housing development (Keel 1976). These revealed a complicated history of mound construction, an underlying late Pigeon–early Connestee phase village midden, evidence of communal ceremonialism, and links to the Hopewell phenomenon of the Ohio and Illinois River valleys.

The first stage of mound construction is represented by a base deposit of yellow clay with a maximum thickness of 50 cm and horizontal dimensions of 12 × 18 m. Some sort of structure was then placed on this surface, as evidence by many post holes. Due to disturbances to this surface by later mound construction activities and the looting of the mound by artifact hunters, a pattern could not be discerned among the post holes to determine the shape of the structure. However, a layer of burned soil and ash on the surface from which the post holes originated suggests that the structure was burned. Above this was deposited approximately 30 cm of a mix of dark brown and gray clayey loam with evidence of individual "basket loads." This surface also supported a post-in-ground structure of indiscernible shape and dimensions. This mound surface, like Biltmore Mound, contained a very large central post; the excavated posthole measured over 60 cm in diameter and 70 cm deep (Keel 1976). Radiocarbon dates on materials associated with this mound phase range between 184 and 360 CE, placing it in the early Connestee phase. The top layers of the mound had been truncated by modern plowing, but a layer of mound slump found on the periphery suggests a cap of dark brown soil. A radiocarbon date from a feature extending from this deposit indicates an approximate terminus of mound use around 390 CE. In essence, this mound appears to have been deliberately layered with variably colored and sourced sediments in a similar fashion to that of the somewhat later Biltmore Mound.

All indications are that Garden Creek Mound No. 2 was very similar to Biltmore mound and, likewise, functioned as a ritual construction, possibly connected with earth renewal and solstice celebrations. Also found at Garden Creek were small blades of Flint Ridge chalcedony, quartz crystals, cut mica, anthropomorphic clay figurines, and numerous animal remains. The later, however, were not nearly as numerous or well preserved as those of the Biltmore Mound. Remains of white-tailed deer, wild turkey, and black bear were the most abundant (Whyte 2011).

Additional investigations involving geophysical surveys and

excavations were conducted in 2011–2012 to shed further light on the site and its role in ritual and social connections within the larger Southeast (Wright 2019). Both ground-penetrating radar and magnetic field gradiometry revealed the presence of an additional mound (No. 4) and two rectangular enclosures with rounded corners just to the east of Mound No. 2. Test excavations over one of the enclosures revealed an outer wall composed of a ditch containing a line of post holes that had been back-filled with river cobbles (Wright 2019). At Garden Creek Mound No. 2 and at the Biltmore Mound, post holes were discovered that had been back-filled with yellow alluvial sand (Keel 1976; Kimball et al. 2010). The use of items from a water source in the back-filling of post holes may have been symbolic. Alternatively, this may have been done to facilitate the rediscovery and re-excavation of these post holes in preparation for ritual annual reconstruction of the structures in association with solstice or world-renewal ceremonies.

Summary

The Middle Woodland period of the Appalachian Summit marks the beginning of a distinct cultural division in which the region encompassing the headwaters of the Little Tennessee and French Broad rivers to the southwest contains evidence of permanent residence, mounds, and participation in exchange and rituals linked to Hopewellian culture in the Ohio River valley. Sites such as the Biltmore Mound and Village and Garden Creek Mound No. 2 and its associated village have yielded evidence of ritualized landscapes involving mound and earth-lodge construction, feasting, and hosting of community rituals related to world renewal and astronomical events. This was evidently due to contact with influential groups to the west of the Appalachians and control over resources, especially the mica that those groups needed for their ritual lives. The construction of rectangular architecture and communal structures such as mounds and earth lodges, and participation in long-distance exchange with Hopewellian societies in the Ohio Valley suggest a gradual increase in social complexity and inequality.

In contrast, northwestern North Carolina, at the headwaters of the Watauga, New, and Yadkin rivers, remained a place of seasonal visitation and transhumance (people passing through), the evidence of which consists of small, temporary encampments lacking evidence of architecture and containing only traces of quotidian domestic life—pottery,

6. Middle Woodland Period: 200–900 CE

stone tools, and food remains. These sites are relatively uncommon in comparison to Early and Late Woodland period sites; it is possible that Hopewellian influences and a greater emphasis on horticulture in the Middle Woodland period dissuaded humans from exploiting the higher elevations in the few centuries leading up to the Medieval Warm climatic period (900 CE).

The Hopewell phenomenon came to an end shortly after 600 CE. Coincidentally, there is evidence from tree-ring data of a fifty-year drought in the Southeast that lasted from 625–725 CE (Stahle et al. 1988). Some sites in the Southeast dating to this period, at the end of the Middle Woodland, show evidence of endemic warfare, nutritional stress, and possibly cannibalism (Whyte 2016). This drought may have contributed to the collapse of Hopewell and adoption of maize horticulture.

7

Late Woodland Period: 900–1400 CE

The spacing of her contractions told her that it was time to leave her village and to follow the narrow, rocky path along the river to the small rockshelter where she'd had her previous two children. It was south-facing and warmed by the sun. If her labors lasted into the night a small fire is all she would need this late in the spring. The shallow river that gently babbled below the shelter was drinkable and would be the water in which she would dunk her baby; the shock of the chilly water would expand its lungs and give it a strong life. The rockshelter, a hole in the earth, for her symbolized a womb—a place of birth and rebirth and a portal through which the living could communicate with ancestor spirits and through which they could pass into the spirit world, and vice versa. This included humans, animals, plants, and objects.

She was twenty years old. Her older sister was her only company, her midwife, if needed. The path to the shelter was an easy one, well-trodden and level. They had to stop only a few times to let contractions pass. They carried extra blankets and cloth to wash and comfort the newborn. They also had two small clay pots—one for water and one for cooking beans and hominy, and a few chert flakes, a bone awl, and some cordage, should a need arise.

Their village, situated on a broad, flat terrace of the river, was circular and consisted of a palisade of posts set in the ground and interwoven with branches and vines. There were entryways on the riverside and at the back. The palisade was more a fence than a fortification. It merely defined what was the village and what was not. Just within the palisade were twelve bark-covered circular houses that looked like inverted baskets from a distance. Smoke constantly issued from a hole in the roof of each. The houses encircled an open area where the people enjoyed games, dances, and ceremonies, and where children and dogs were always running about. Behind the village and along the large creek that

7. Late Woodland Period: 900–1400 CE

flowed into the river just below it are the gardens where they had just planted maize and squash.

The two women arrived at the shelter just as the sun was setting behind a ridge. They gathered some sticks for a fire and started it with some tinder and an ember that they had brought from their hearth, and the older one filled the pots with water and began cooking, while the other paced, panted, and chanted. The labor was a long one, lasting through the night and well into the next day. Although her sister tried to comfort and sustain her, the mother grew very weak and feverish, the contractions ceased, and she and her baby died.

The sister returned to the village alone to announce the sad news. The village healer and relatives of the young woman then went to the rockshelter before sunset to free her spirit from her body and to bury her where she died. The sound of the river echoed off the stony shelter wall as the sister and her nephews began to dig. Creating a grave was easy; simply by removing several large rocks and the soil in-between they created a hole sufficiently deep and wide. They gently placed her in the grave in a flexed position on her right side with her head resting on a large flat rock, as though she was sleeping. Her head was positioned toward the opening of the shelter to represent rebirth from the womb of the earth. Her face presented toward the place of the rising sun. A bone awl and a basket of dried beans and maize kernels were placed by her hands so she could find and use them in the spirit world, lamentations were expressed, and the body was then covered with soil and rocks.

******

By approximately 900 CE, much of the northern hemisphere began to experience a slight warming known as the Medieval Warm period (Fagan 2008). Temperatures ultimately increased to the degree that farmers in England and other parts of northern Europe expanded into and cultivated lands at higher altitudes and latitudes. It also allowed the Norse to travel the North Atlantic and establish settlements in Greenland and Newfoundland. This is the first time that we see permanent villages and maize cultivation above 2,500 feet in the Appalachian Summit (Whyte 2003). Permanent settlement was also made possible by the introduction of a new hybrid cultigen—flint maize, which is more resistant to freezing than its predecessors. Maize was first domesticated in central Mexico approximately 7,000 years ago and gradually made its way into the southeastern United States around 800 CE. Its widespread adoption may have been catalyzed by a fifty-year drought that affected much of the Southeast between 675 and 725 CE (see Stahle et al. 1988).

Dozens of high-elevation residential sites dating to between 1000 and 1450 CE have been identified in the Appalachian Summit, but few have been excavated. The first permanent residents were probably descended from Early and Middle Woodland people who had previously occupied the uplands only seasonally. The new villagers had become dependent upon maize horticulture as a nutritional buffer and storable food that enabled and required sedentary settlement through the winter months. Their diets, however, remained focused on wild meats, nuts and vegetables. In the lowlands to the south and west, however, societies had become dependent upon maize *agriculture*, providing a diet with a greater emphasis on cultivated foods and supplemented with wild foods. Later in this period, by approximately 1350 CE, beans (also a Mexican domesticate) were introduced to the region. The combination of beans and maize provided a complete protein. At a small rockshelter called Stillhouse Hollow Cave in western Watauga County, North Carolina, a hearth was found that contained the pieces of a broken clay jar and carbonized maize kernels and beans (Whyte 2015). One of the bean fragments was radiocarbon dated to 1350 CE. This may be archaeological evidence of a ritual that was practiced by the Cherokee Indians in historic times (Whyte 2019): "the conjurer takes some of the grains of seven ears of corn and feeds the fire, i.e., burns them.... In a like manner they observe the same custom before eating the bean when it fills in the hull" (Witthoft 1949:32).

Artifacts of the Late Woodland Period

Late Woodland period pottery in the northern part of the Appalachian Summit consists mostly of globular jar forms with rounded or slightly conical bases, constricted necks, and thickened, punctated rims (Figure 7.1). The locally derived clay was usually mixed with coarse sand or "grit," or with crushed rock such as quartz, gneiss, schist, soapstone, or limestone. The broken vessel in the hearth at Stillhouse Hollow Cave (Whyte 2015) was tempered with crushed limestone, indicating the possibility that it was made many kilometers to the west where limestone naturally occurs. Vessels were constructed by a combination of molding and coiling (Whyte 2017a). The exteriors of vessels were sometimes smoothed but more often textured with net impressions or

7. Late Woodland Period: 900–1400 CE

stamped with a wooden paddle on which rectilinear designs or symbols were carved (Figure 7.2). The thickened rims were always decorated or symboled with punctations made with fingertips, feather quills, sticks, or with spatulate tools that left leaf-like shapes in the clay (Whyte et al. 2011). These marks often formed chevron shapes that undoubtedly had meaning for the makers, users, and viewers of the pottery (Figure 7.3).

This style of pottery may have been copied from more complex societies in the southern part of the Appalachian Summit, near present-day Asheville, who were participating in what is known as "Mississippian culture." These groups, known as "Pisgah phase"

Figure 7.1. Partially reconstructed Late Woodland ceramic jar from the Katie Griffith site, Watauga County, North Carolina.

Figure 7.2. Late Woodland net-impressed (left) and rectilinear-stamped (right) pottery.

Figure 7.3. Late Woodland pottery rim sherds from the Ward Site, Watauga County, North Carolina.

societies, constructed platform mounds and rectangular houses much like their Middle Woodland predecessors, practiced more intensive maize horticulture, participated in long-distance exchange of marine shell and other items, and probably were organized into chiefdoms (Dickens 1976). In other words, the Appalachian Summit of Western North Carolina continued to be "split" between the headwaters of the Little Tennessee and French Broad and those of the Watauga, New, and Yadkin rivers. Residents of the former were heavily influenced by more complex Mississippian societies to the south and west, while the latter remained egalitarian woodland villagers similar to their contemporaries on the Piedmont to the east and were only marginally influenced by Mississippian culture. The Late Woodland pottery of northwestern North Carolina, although Pisgah-like, shares manufacturing traits with Dan River phase pottery (Coe and Lewis 1952) of the Piedmont to the east; it has not yet been given a type name.

Stone technologies of the Late Woodland period varied little from their Middle Woodland antecedents. Larger manos and metátes made from unmodified river cobbles were likely used to process maize and nutmeats. Small arrow points of chert, quartz, and chalcedony occur in two forms: triangular and serrated triangular (Figure 7.4). Some of the

7. Late Woodland Period: 900–1400 CE

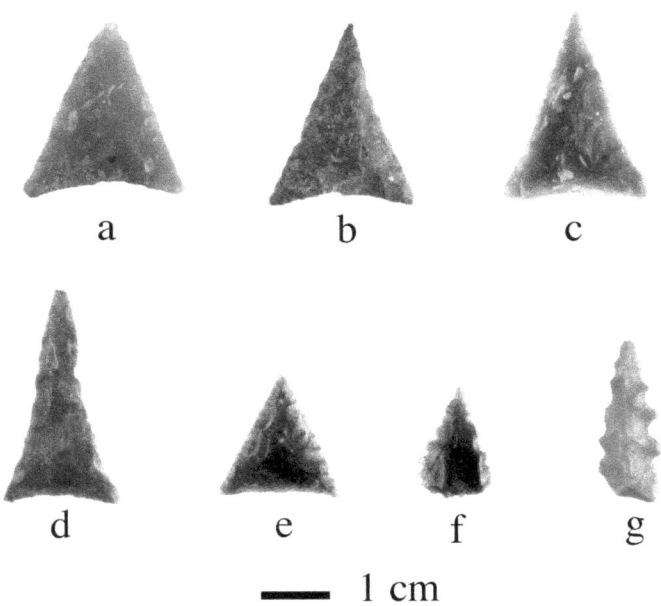

Figure 7.4. Late Woodland arrow points.

latter, known as "Pisgah points," are best described as serrated "slugs" with poorly formed bases that may have been glued loosely to the ends of cane shafts. One possibility is that these were reserved for warfare, as removal of the shaft from a body would likely leave the serrated point embedded. In addition to these tools and weaponry, flake tools with variously shaped edges were used for cutting, scraping, drilling, planing, and sawing of a variety of materials. Small axe blades or "celts" made of greenstone and hafted in wooden handles were used as axes and possibly weapons (Figure 7.5). These were not grooved like the earlier forms of the Late Archaic period. Instead, they tapered from the blade to the poll and thus were socketed in a hole through the end of a wooden handle.

Other interesting artifacts of this period include clay and soapstone tobacco pipes, beads and other ornaments made from imported marine shell, and large stone disks (Figure 7.6) that may have been used in chunkey, a game in which javelins were thrown at the place where the rolling disk was predicted to stop (Hudson 1976). Small ground stone and pottery disks (Figure 7.7) found on residential sites of this period may have been used in a game similar to one played by the Iroquois

Left: **Figure 7.5. Late Woodland greenstone celts.** *Right:* **Figure 7.6. Late Woodland chunkey stone.**

Figure 7.7. Late Woodland disks made from pottery sherds.

known as "the deer button game" wherein "eight buttons, about an inch in diameter, were made of elk-horn, and having been rounded and polished, were slightly burned upon one side to blacken them" (Morgan 1962:302). These were employed in a gambling game not unlike craps, a game played with dice today. The Cherokee, Creek, and Choctaw played a similar game involving charred beans or corn (Hudson 1976: 426).

Mountain Life in the Late Woodland Period

The first experiments in permanent settlement in northwestern North Carolina appear in the Late Woodland period. The most

7. Late Woodland Period: 900–1400 CE

thoroughly investigated village is the Ward site, located at the confluence of Cove Creek and Watauga River, and the slightly later Katie Griffith site along Pine Orchard Creek near Todd (Whyte 2003). These sites are discussed at length below. There were undoubtedly several small villages along the headwaters of the Watauga and New rivers, but they remain to be discovered and investigated. Some communities were nucleated villages in which houses were clustered and surrounded by a palisade (the Ward site), while others may have been isolated farmsteads or clusters of farmsteads linked together in a dispersed settlement (the Katie Griffith site) (Figure 7.8). Evidence of the Late Woodland period is also found in rockshelters such as Church Rockshelter Nos. 1 and 2 and Stillhouse Hollow Cave, and on various upland landforms such as toe slopes, ridges, gaps, and saddles (Purrington 1983). These tend to be smaller, temporary-use sites with few artifacts and no evidence of structures.

Subsistence evidence, found mostly on residential sites and in rockshelters where organic materials are better preserved, indicates

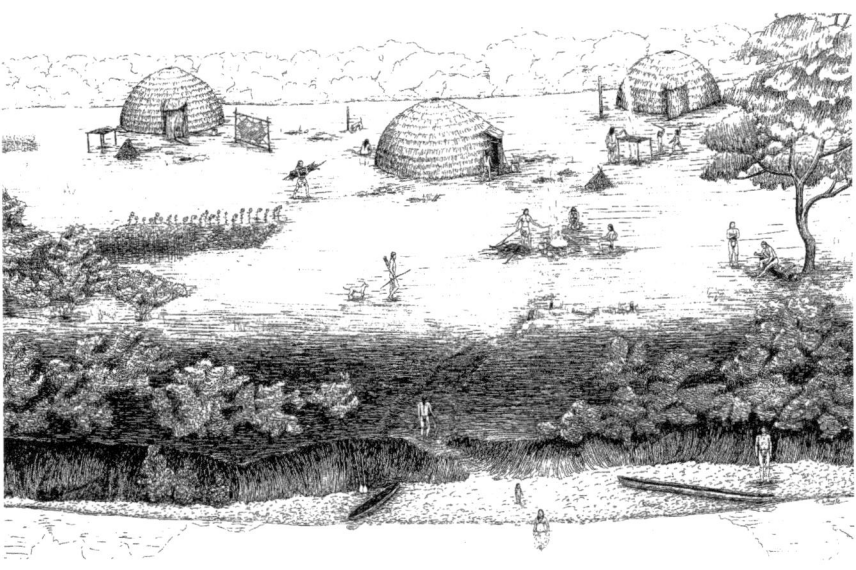

Figure 7.8. Artist's reconstruction of a Late Woodland period hamlet (courtesy of the Frank H. McClung Museum of Natural History & Culture, University of Tennessee, Knoxville; drawing by Tom Whyte).

a continued focus on hunted and gathered wild foods but with an increased emphasis (over the preceding Middle Woodland period) on the three primary domesticates—maize, squash, and beans. At the Ward site, several contexts yielded pieces of carbonized maize cupules (cob) and kernels; however, no beans were recovered, probably because the main village occupation immediately predates the introduction of beans to the region, which occurred after 1300 CE. The archaeobotanical materials from this site remain to be studied by a trained archaeobotanist to determine the entire array of plant foods and medicine represented.

Late Woodland period human burials have been found in villages, rockshelters and caves. The poorly preserved skeletal remains of a young adult (possibly male) were found in an oval pit a few meters outside the village wall at the Ward site. This individual was buried in a flexed position with a greenstone celt. The burial may predate the village occupation.

One burial dating to this period was discovered in 1968 in Church Rockshelter No. 1 and excavated by the landowner and an ASU biologist (Whyte 2013b). The individual, a woman of approximately 20 years of age, was reported to have been buried in a flexed position with the head toward the rockshelter opening and Watauga River. Excavation of the site in 2003 revealed the presence of perinatal human remains scattered within the backdirt of the 1968 excavations (screens had not been used). It was determined that the infant remains may have been associated with the young adult remains (perhaps *in utero*) and that the cause of death of each was childbirth (Whyte 2013b). A very similar pattern of burial was observed at the roughly contemporaneous Hidden Valley Rockshelter site in mountainous Virginia (Whyte 2007b). There, skeletal remains of a pre-teen human of unknown sex were found in the same fetal position with the head toward the shelter opening. Three dog skulls were encountered in the grave fill above the human remains; dogs for many Native Americans represented guides to the spirit world (Kerber 1997).

Not far to the west of Boone there is abundant evidence of burial of humans in caves, which served as natural tombs. Artifact collectors vandalized one such cave, Lake Hole Cave in Cherokee National Forest, northeastern Tennessee, in the early 1990s (Whyte and Kimball 1997). At the request of the Eastern Band of Cherokee Indians archaeologists excavated the vandalized deposits and recovered the scattered and broken skeletal remains of approximately 100 people, including males, females, and individuals of all ages. Also recovered were arrow points,

7. Late Woodland Period: 900–1400 CE

pieces of pottery, thousands of marine shell beads, and bone tools that had been buried with the dead. One bone tool was radiocarbon dated to 1260 CE. In the meantime, nine men were arrested and convicted for violating the Archaeological Resources Protection Act, which was passed in 1969 to protect cultural resources on Federal lands. The sheer number of humans buried in the cave indicates that cave burial was a preferred method of interment in the region in the thirteenth century. This may explain why no burials were encountered within the Ward site village confines.

Further to the south late precontact village sites such as the Warren Wilson site east of Asheville, often contain shaft-and-chamber burials located in and around the houses (Dickens 1976). These were constructed by creating an underground burial chamber. The body and mortuary offerings were placed in the chamber, which was then sealed with rocks or wood, and the access shaft filled with soil. This burial method effectively created a "cave" to contain the body.

One of these was also found on Wagner Island, now submerged in Watauga Reservoir (Boyd 1986). In winter 1983/84 the reservoir was partially drained by the Tennessee Valley Authority to make repairs on the dam. During the drawdown, archaeologists located and investigated many ancient sites that had been submerged since the dam was completed in 1948. Excavations on Wagner Island, a former island of the Watauga River, exposed the remains (post molds) of a house and various other features, including the shaft-and-chamber grave. No human skeletal remains were preserved in the grave. However, a large piece of mica and a cluster of large chalcedony flakes were found in the base of the grave, and large river cobbles had been used to seal the chamber from the shaft. Also recovered from the grave fill that resulted from collapse of the chamber include a Pisgah style clay pipe and several pottery sherds with punctated, thickened rims similar to those found on Late Woodland sites in northwestern North Carolina.

The Ward Site

The Ward site is a Late Woodland period palisaded village located on the west bank of Watauga River just upstream of its confluence with Cove Creek in Watauga County. Although the site was occupied many times, the village probably dates to between 1000 and 1300 CE. A cabin was built on the site, probably by Benjamin Ward, between 1780 and

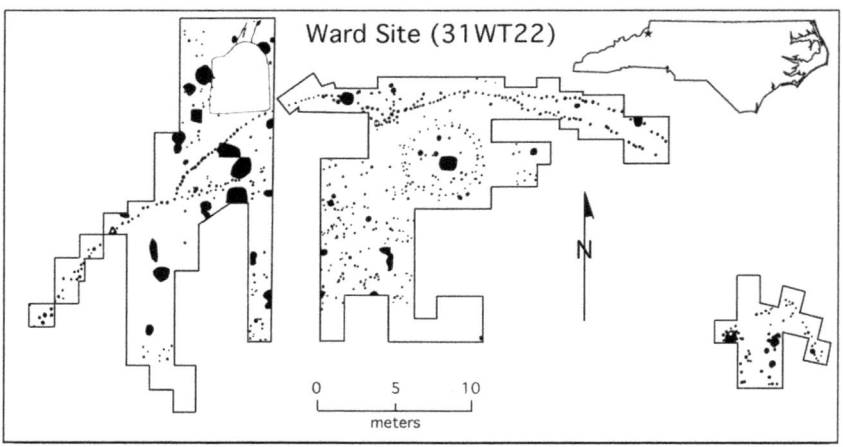

Figure 7.9. Map of the Ward site features and post holes, Watauga County, North Carolina.

1790. Archaeological investigations of the site were undertaken by ASU from 1971 to 1974, and in 1982 and 1990 (Whyte 2003). In all, 1455 square meters of plowzone and underlying midden were excavated in five-foot squares and trenches to expose the northern half of a circular palisaded village. Over 200 post holes of a single-wall palisade form an arc suggesting a roughly 52-meter diameter enclosure (Figure 7.9). Other features of the village that were excavated include one human burial, several hearths and pit features, and the post holes and central hearth of a circular house. This structure consisted of a double-posted wall measuring 5 meters in diameter (Figure 7.10). Its shape, sturdy construction, and central hearth imply that the village was occupied year-round. Other post holes and hearths concentrated just within the palisade but forming less defined clusters undoubtedly belonged to similar structures and suggest a typical eastern woodlands village pattern with circular houses surrounding a plaza area. Post holes of a possible rectangular structure lacking a hearth were found on the western edge of the site. Since its post hole pattern overlaps the earlier village palisade this structure likely dates to a later period of occupation of the site.

The nearly 20,000 pottery sherds recovered from the Ward site represent a variety of wares and time periods. The vast majority resulted from the Late Woodland village occupation, and represent primarily

7. Late Woodland Period: 900–1400 CE

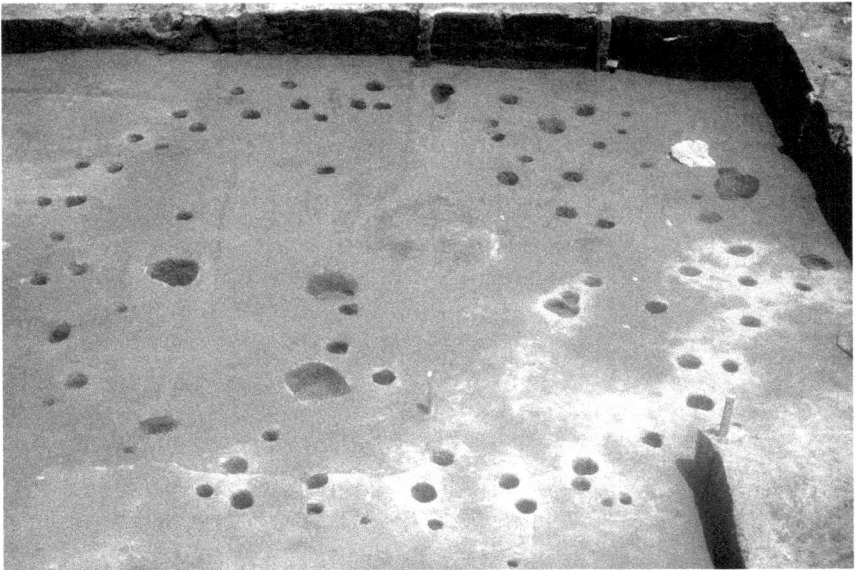

Figure 7.10. Remains of a circular house at the Ward site, Watauga County, North Carolina.

medium to large jar forms with subconical to rounded bases, constricted necks, and thickened punctated rims. Tempering agents include crushed biotite schist, crushed quartz, crushed limestone, and grit. Vessel exteriors were primarily net impressed or rectilinear stamped. Vessel interiors were smoothed or coarsely scraped.

Lithic artifacts recovered include the usual suite of chipped stone debitage and tools, ground stone celts, and cobble tools such as manos, metátes, hammers, and anvils. Chipped stone artifacts were made from locally derived quartz and chert, chalcedony, and jasper from VRP sources located over 32 kilometers downriver. Projectile points associated with the village include small isosceles triangular forms and serrated Pisgah types.

Animal remains associated with the village component are few and very poorly preserved. Plant remains include maize kernel and cupule. One feature (21) contained numerous cupule (cob) fragments and abundant wood charcoal, samples of each yielding radiocarbon assays post-dating the village occupation by three or four hundred years. This means that Feature 21 probably dates to a 16th or 17th-century occupation of the site, long after the village had been abandoned.

The Katie Griffith Site

In spring 1998, landowners discovered artifacts while digging the foundation footers for a barn near Todd, North Carolina. The Katie Griffith site is situated on a north-facing alluvial fan adjacent to Pine Orchard Creek, which flows into the South Fork of the New River at Todd, North Carolina. The site was used many times by migratory hunter-gatherers between 10,000 and 1,000 years ago. A permanent residence was there in the Late Woodland period, at approximately 1350 CE.

Four seasons (spring 1998, 1999, 2001, and 2013) of salvage excavations were conducted by ASU archaeological field schools (Whyte 2017b). The first season focused on the interior of the barn foundation and a small area adjacent to the barn's northwestern wall. In the two subsequent seasons, when the landowners planned to grade the area for better access to the newly constructed barn, excavation of this latter area was expanded. The final season (2013) focused on excavation of a single feature (Feature 6) and its immediate surrounds.

Excavation profiles uphill and immediately northwest of the barn wall revealed four observable soil strata distinguishable by color and texture. From the surface down, these are: a mottled historically redeposited colluvium of varying thickness; a historic plowzone of dark brown sandy loam that contained a mix of historic and precontact artifacts; a very dark brown sandy loam "midden" containing only precontact artifacts; and a yellow-brown sandy clay loam containing few artifacts and extending to an unknown depth. Surfaces of ancient cultural features were observed immediately below the plowzone and midden zones.

Found within and immediately northwest of the barn were the burned remains of a fourteenth-century structure and artifacts and features dating from the Early Archaic through Late Woodland periods. Although only partly uncovered, the structural remains include post holes, concentrations of fired daub, scatters of wood charcoal, patches of carbonized bark and wood, and an assortment of associated features (Figure 7.11). Some of the post holes, like those observed at Middle Woodland mound sites in western North Carolina, such as Garden Creek Mound No. 2 and the Biltmore Mound, had been back-filled with yellow alluvial sand. The structure may have been roughly circular and appears to have been constructed of wattle and daub. These structural remains lay above and below various thicknesses of midden. At the

7. Late Woodland Period: 900–1400 CE

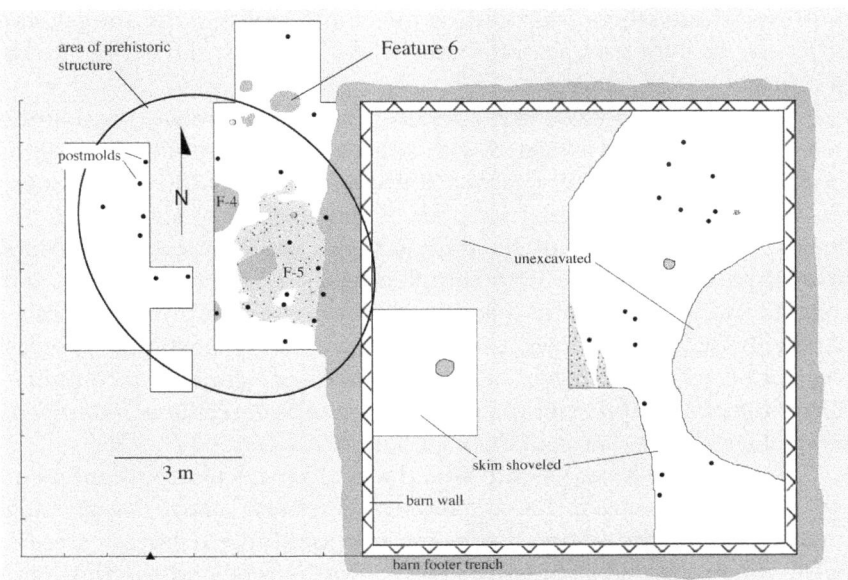

Figure 7.11. Map of the Katie Griffith site features and post holes, Watauga County, North Carolina.

base of the lower midden were artifacts typologically dated mostly to the Middle Archaic through Early and Middle Woodland periods. Feature 6, located immediately east of the structure, was a deep, bell shaped food storage pit, the bottom of which had been lined with large pottery sherds and wood charcoal (Figure 7.12). The pottery and charcoal may have served

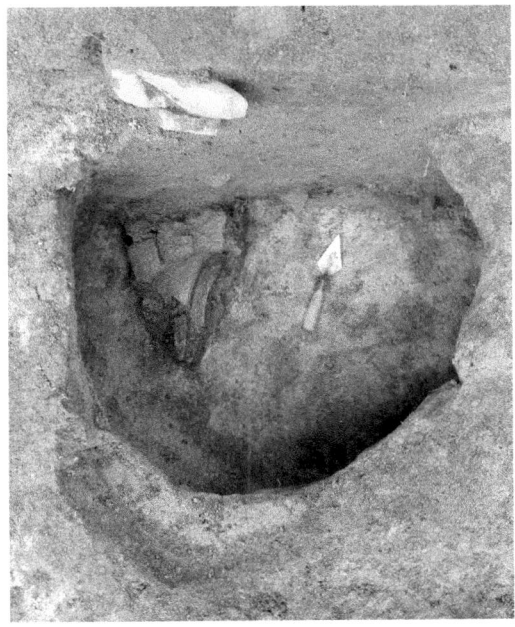

Figure 7.12. Feature 6, Katie Griffith Site, Watauga County, North Carolina.

to prevent food stores from getting moist and moldy. After the pit was no longer used for storage it was filled with soil, rocks, and various kinds of refuse.

The Late Woodland structure represents an isolated residence that may have been associated with a dispersed community along Pine Orchard Creek and other nearby tributaries of the South Fork. Numerous radiocarbon dates securely place its occupation at about 1350 CE. Pottery from this Late Woodland period occupation includes fragments of medium-to-large jars with rounded bases, constricted necks, and collared and punctated rims (Figure 7.1). Vessels were formed by a combination of molding (the bases) and coiling (upper vessel portions). The clay was tempered with crushed quartz, crushed soapstone, or a combination of the two. Vessel exteriors were net-impressed, rectilinear-stamped, scraped, or a combination of these (Whyte 2017a, 2017b).

Much of the Katie Griffith site, thanks to conscientious landowners, remains preserved. Its archaeological record is surprisingly rich for a small, north-facing alluvial fan overlooking a tributary stream in the mountains. Possible explanations for its repeated use throughout the Holocene Epoch are that it was located along a well-established trail linking the New and Watauga River valleys and it is in a place where important lithic (soapstone), food, and perhaps medicinal resources were abundant. Once established as a place where migratory hunter-gatherers could easily meet the needs of their survival, the site would have been revisited, perhaps seasonally, by subsequent generations. Ultimately, during the Medieval Warm period when permanent residences were established in the region, it was recognized as an ideal location for a farmstead. Possibly due to the onset of the Little Ice Age, the residence was abandoned by 1400 CE.

Lake Hole Cave

In March 1990 a Cherokee National Forest (CNF) employee was walking through the woods on a hillside overlooking Watauga Reservoir in Johnson County, Tennessee, when he came across a hole, just big enough for a human to crawl through, in the rocky embankment. Strewn below the hole were human bones and teeth, and aluminum cans, cigarette butts, and other trash. Recognizing that an archaeological site located on federal lands was being illegally explored, he contacted CNF law enforcement and archaeologists to alert them of the crime. When

7. Late Woodland Period: 900–1400 CE

they went to the site to assess the damage, they found excavation equipment, a bag of marijuana, and a trash bag containing human skulls just inside the small entrance to the cave. Realizing that the perpetrators would return to commence their digging (and smoking!), law enforcement officers went to the site before daylight on the next Saturday morning, hid themselves beneath the leaves near the pathway leading down to the site, and waited. It was not long before they heard a vehicle park, doors shut, and men walking and talking on their way to the cave. After a while, the officers went down to the cave and arrested three men for violation of the Archaeological Resources Protection Act (ARPA). Ultimately, nine men were arrested and charged with misdemeanor and felony violations.

Follow-up investigations at the site by Cherokee National Forest archaeologists revealed that the small opening immediately led to two cave chambers, a small one spiraling down a few meters to the left, and a larger one extending about a dozen meters to the right. The cave had formed by water dissolving the dolomite bedrock over many millennia. The right chamber was large enough for an adult to stand upright, while the left chamber was little more than a narrow crawl space. Both chambers contained earthen floors exhibiting numerous, overlapping potholes. Human and animal bones and modern litter were scattered about. The vandals clearly had severely disturbed or destroyed an ancient human burial site.

At the request of the Eastern Band of Cherokee Indians, archaeologists from Appalachian State University were asked to carefully and reverently excavate the disturbed deposits and recover human remains and artifacts from them (Whyte and Kimball 1997). These investigations would ultimately play a role in the prosecution of the vandals. The excavations took place from May through July 1991. All excavated fill from the site was hauled in feedbags uphill to a vehicle and brought to Appalachian State University for wet screening. Ultimately, approximately 24 cubic meters of soil were removed and processed.

It was discovered that the vandals that had been arrested, and possibly many others, had been disturbing the site for a long time and to the point that they were excavating through each other's backdirt. Archaeologists were able to determine which deposits had been disturbed by discovering cigarette butts, batteries, food wrappers, et cetera, among the human remains. No undisturbed human burials were encountered in their excavations—only scattered and mostly fragmentary human remains, many exhibiting shovel marks.

Boone Before Boone

In all, over 12,000 human bones and teeth representing approximately 136 individuals were recovered. The remains were those of individuals of all ages and both sexes; however, there was a notable paucity of skull parts undoubtedly because of the collection of skulls by the site's vandals. Also recovered were over 6,000 marine shell beads, 17 bone beads, 8 bone and antler tools, 136 pottery sherds, 25 triangular arrow points, and 67 chalcedony and chert flakes (Whyte and Kimball 1997). One bone tool, probably representing a burial offering, with permission of the Eastern Band of Cherokee Indians, was submitted for radiocarbon dating. The resulting assay was approximately 1260 CE.

Marine shell beads recovered include small disk shapes manufactured from the outer whorls of whelk (probably lightning whelk; *Sinistrofulgur perversum*) shells, and ones made by removing the spires of *Olivia*, and *Marginella* snail shells. Undoubtedly, countless other beads had been recovered and removed by the site's vandals. These beads were probably manufactured by residents of the Gulf or South Atlantic coasts and traded from group to group until they were buried as necklaces and other ornaments adorning the bodies placed in Lake Hole Cave.

The pottery sherds recovered may be the scattered remains of whole vessels that had been buried with individuals or parts of vessels that had contained burning fuel to light the cave during times of interment. A minimum of four vessels is represented and exhibit smoothed-over rectilinear stamping and plain surfaces typical of thirteenth-century sites in the region. The arrow points recovered are mostly made of local chert, chalcedony, and jasper and most are broken. Breakage and evidence of impact fractures and bone and meat polish on several specimens suggest that many of the points had been embedded in bodies interred in the cave (Kimball 2019).

There is no telling what the vandals had removed from the cave. No artifacts that may have come from the site were found among their possessions at the times of the arrests. The bag of skulls that had been stored just inside the entrance had been removed prior to the arrests at the site. Although it is tragic that an archaeological site of such importance had been disturbed, it is much more devastating that a burial place sacred to contemporary Native Americans was so selfishly violated. Another tragedy is that the site also was home to important paleontological remains. The ASU excavations resulted in recovery of remains of extinct Pleistocene horse (*Equus* sp.), beautiful armadillo (*Dasypus bellus*), and possibly dire wolf (*Canis dirus*).

7. Late Woodland Period: 900–1400 CE

Ultimately, all of the human remains and artifacts were given to the Eastern Band of Cherokee Indians for ceremonious reburial. The cave has been sealed and hopefully protected from further damage. The nine vandals have paid their fines and served their incarceration times. Unfortunately, there is much about the site that could not be determined because of the damage that had been done. Questions that remain are: For how long was the cave used as a burial place? Were bodies placed on the surface in the cave or were they buried? How were bodies distributed in the cave? Were males, females, adults, and children treated similarly? Were certain artifacts associated with one sex, one age, group, or another? Were the individuals interred members of local communities? What did the vandals remove from the site? These are questions that can only be answered by archaeology when things are found in undisturbed contexts.

Summary

The Medieval Warm period, enjoyed by native highlanders for about 500 years, came to an end with a vengeance at about 1400 CE. This was the onset of the "Little Ice Age," which was not truly an ice age but a measurably cooler period that lasted until the Industrial Revolution (approximately 1850) when humans effected global warming with carbon pollutants. Year-round residence, such as at the Ward and Katie Griffith sites was no longer sustainable at the higher elevations. Undoubtedly, crops failed due to late spring and early autumn frosts, and food stores were insufficient for surviving the harsher winters. No permanent native residential sites above 2500 feet and dating to the Little Ice Age have yet been discovered; the northwestern counties of North Carolina appear to have been abandoned except for occasional seasonal visits or transhumance through the area.

At lower elevations large villages such as the Coweeta Creek site in Macon County, North Carolina, and the Plum Grove site in Washington County, Tennessee, were occupied repeatedly in the early centuries of the Little Ice Age. Coweeta Creek, located along the Little Tennessee River near Franklin, North Carolina, was a Qualla phase village with rectangular houses surrounding a plaza (Rodning 2008). It was first occupied at around 1450 CE. This precontact occupation of the site probably consisted of a palisaded (fortified) village much like that of the Warren Wilson site. However, the mound at Coweeta Creek resulted from the burning and rebuilding of six council house structures on the same spot (Ward and Davis 1999). The council house and surrounding domiciles were square with rounded corners and had southeast-facing entrances. European trade items were associated with all but the first council house deposits and few were found in other village contexts on the site. This suggests that the village was largely abandoned by the time of European contact, its occupants dispersing into individual farmsteads, but the council house remained a place of communal gatherings until 1838 CE, when most of the Cherokee were forced to relocate to Oklahoma (Rodning 2008).

The proto-historic and historic period occupations of Coweeta Creek are associated with the Qualla phase, proven to be an archaeological manifestation of the Cherokee. Qualla pottery, one artifactual signature of the phase, is tempered with grit (Figure 7.13). Jar forms were most often stamped on the exterior with a curvilinear design and rims were often finished with a pinched folded rim or rim strip (Rodning 2008). Bowl forms were smoothed or burnished on the exteriors and the upper portions incised with a series of lines forming geometric patterns (Figure 7.14). This incising, known as the "Lamar" style, indicates influence by societies residing to the south in northern Georgia (Rodning 2008).

Burke pottery, found mostly at sites in the upper Catawba River valley, such as the Berry site (discussed in the next chapter), is very similar but tempered with crushed soapstone (Keeler 1971; Moore 1999). Jar forms were typically stamped on the exterior with a distinctive curvilinear pattern, often showing impressions of the wood grain of the paddle

Figure 7.13. Curvilinear-stamped Qualla vessel fragment from Garden Creek Mound No. 1, Haywood County, North Carolina (courtesy of the Research Laboratories of Archaeology, University of North Carolina at Chapel Hill).

7. Late Woodland Period: 900–1400 CE

Figure 7.14. Lamar incised Qualla vessel fragment from the Coweeta Creek site, Macon County, North Carolina (courtesy of the Research Laboratories of Archaeology, University of North Carolina at Chapel Hill).

used as a stamp (Figure 7.15). Bowl forms exhibit Lamar incising similar to that of Qualla pottery.

To date, no Qualla (Cherokee) ceramics have been found in the northwestern counties of North Carolina. This suggests that the

Figure 7.15. Curvilinear-stamped Burke pottery from Church Rockshelter No. 1, Watauga County, North Carolina.

northern extent of Cherokee occupation in the Appalachian Summit was approximately demarcated by the Toe River in Mitchell and Yancey Counties.

The Plum Grove site, located along the Nolichucky River near Erwin, Tennessee, was originally thought also to be a Qualla phase village because Lamar incised ceramics were recovered along with European trade items (Dickens n.d.). And, because some of the trade items found at the site were thought to have been of 16th-century Spanish origin, it also was considered a possible candidate for the town of Guasili visited by de Soto in 1540 (Beck 1997). Subsequent investigations at the site (Boyd 1987; Whyte 1994; Whyte and Boyd 2019), however, have shown that the ceramic assemblage, now referred to as that of the "Nolichucky phase," is more akin to the Burke series originating at the headwaters of the Yadkin and Catawba rivers in the eastern foothills of the Blue Ridge in North Carolina. Also, the European trade items recovered (primarily glass beads) are now known to be of later English origin (Marcoux 2012). The historic occupation of the Plum Grove site has been securely dated to the latter half of the 17th century (Whyte and Boyd 2019).

The Woodland period came to an end with gradual exposure to European invaders. European trade goods such as beads, knives, mirrors and guns made their way to most of the natives of the region long before there were any sightings of the white humans. But even these material items had a profound impact on the lives, social structures, and inter-tribal relationships of native groups in the Appalachian Summit, although little when compared to the impacts of disease and warfare that would soon follow.

Mississippian Influence in the Appalachian Summit

In the more southwestern counties of North Carolina, south of the Toe River, there are large palisaded village sites, some of which include mounds, that date to the late pre-contact period (1200–1600 CE). Like the earlier Biltmore Mound and Garden Creek Mound No. 2, these mounds supported rectangular structures used in ceremonies. The presence of these mounds, village palisades, evidence of long-distance exchange of shell, mica, and copper, evidence of status differentiation, and a sharing of religious iconography indicate connections with more

7. Late Woodland Period: 900–1400 CE

complex societies residing along the Gulf coast and in the Midsouth. This Mississippian cultural influence appears to have had only a marginal impact on native residents of northwestern North Carolina.

This southern Appalachian manifestation of Mississippian influence is known as the "Pisgah phase." In addition to the characteristics listed above, the Pisgah phase is recognized by a distinctive pottery style consisting of bowls and large jar forms. These vessels were most often tempered with coarse sand or grit, the exteriors stamped with rectilinear impressions, and the thickened rims tooled with angular symbols or decorations. Fragments of similar vessels have been found on Late Woodland sites in the northwestern mountains (e.g., the Ward and Katie Griffith sites), but with different tempering materials (Figures 7.1, 7.3). Evidence from these sites, lacking other aspects of the Pisgah phase such as mounds and shell artifacts, indicates only marginal Mississippian influence.

Garden Creek Mound No. 1 overlooking Pigeon River in Haywood County, just west of Asheville, was excavated by UNC–Chapel Hill archaeologists in the 1960s. It was built and used for ceremonial purposes between 1290 and 1420 CE (Schubert 2017). This and other evidence place it in what is known by archaeologists as the Pisgah phase, characterized by villages with palisades and sometimes mounds, distinctive pottery and modes of human burial, and evidence of exchange in marine shell and mica (Dickens 1976). The mound was constructed over a Pisgah phase village that had a palisade with bastions, possibly indicating a regular threat of invasion. The mound exhibits a complicated history of construction involving several building stages and a pair of earth lodges (Dickens 1976). Its overall size was approximately 40 × 45 meters and, after several decades of plowing, stood approximately 2 meters high.

The 23 human burials found within and beneath Garden Creek Mound No. 1 include a mix of males and females of varying ages. Just over half were buried with shell ornaments such as beads, ear pins, and disks or "gorgets" carved from the outer whorls of whelk shells. Only one of the four burials found in the adjacent village contained preserved burial offerings, possibly indicating a higher status among individuals associated with the mound (Dickens 1976).

Nearly 40,000 animal remains representing at least 39 species were recovered from the mound excavations (Whyte 2017c). These include shells of mollusks and bones of fishes, amphibians, reptiles, birds, and mammals. Most numerous were remains of toads, box turtles, wild turkeys, black bears, and deer. Remains of toads and passenger pigeons found among the mound's paired earth lodges appear to represent whole animals (although bones of the head are lacking) and therefore may represent offerings. Deer and bear remains are dominated by meatier parts of the body and include many complete or nearly complete long bones. This and the sheer number of animal remains indicate that feasting occurred on or within the structures on the mound and that individuals of greater status were involved. Another indication is that late in the mound's use, a series of posts was set in the ground to partition the mound from the adjacent village, presumably to distinguish the sacred from secular or the elite from the commoners (Schubert 2017).

The Warren Wilson site, located on the Swannanoa River in Buncombe County, is a palisaded Pisgah phase village lacking a mound (Dickens 1976). Also excavated by UNC archaeologists in the 1960s, this site included several squarish domestic structures located just within the palisade and surrounding a plaza of communal space. The houses measured about 6 meters square, were constructed of posts set in the ground and horizontally woven with wattle, and then probably covered with bark. Four large interior posts probably supported a bark-covered roof. Each house had a raised clay hearth near the center and an entryway, usually at the midpoint of the south wall (Dickens 1976).

Human burials, numbering 35 in all, were concentrated within and around the houses. Some were found beneath the central hearths of houses. Many were shaft-and-chamber burials in which the body was placed in a side or central chamber separated from the grave shaft by a wall of rocks or wood, and then the shaft filled in with soil. This, in essence, created a concavity in which the body rested. Individuals of varying ages and both sexes were represented. Shell gorgets were found only with remains of infants and young children. One adult male was buried in a side-chamber grave with box turtle shell rattles on his ankles (Dickens 1976).

Over 17,000 vertebrate remains were recovered from various deposits on the site. Approximately half of these were identifiable to vertebrate class and include those of fishes, amphibians, reptiles, birds, and mammals. Similar to Garden Creek Mound No. 1, remains of toads, box turtles, turkeys, black bears, and deer are especially abundant (Runquist 1979; Whyte 2017c). One feature identified as a daub-processing pit associated with the village palisade contained the postcranial bones of several toads. A similar feature was found next to the palisade at another Mississippian village, the Coweeta Creek site

7. Late Woodland Period: 900–1400 CE

in Macon County, North Carolina. This feature contained over 17,000 bones of toads, almost none of which were from the head. Referencing a recipe for toad preparation in a Cherokee Cookbook (Ulmer and Beck 1951), Whyte and Compton (2020) argue that the residents of these sites were Cherokee peoples who consumed toads in great numbers in spring. Indeed, the Chickamaugas allegedly referred to the Cherokees of southwestern North Carolina as "frog eaters" (Schwarze 1923). According to the recipe, toads were decapitated and skinned to remove the toxic components prior to consumption (Ulmer and Beck 1951).

Another possible sign of Mississippian influence in the northwestern counties of North Carolina is the presence of petroglyphs similar to those associated with Mississippian Pisgah and Qualla phase sites in the southwestern part of the state (Loubser et al. 2019). One example is Cranberry Rock on the South Fork of the New River in Ashe County (Figure 7.16). This boulder of mica schist contains over 70 cupules (rounded pits) on its surface that were laboriously pecked into shape. The meaning of these cupules is unknown, but rocks containing them as well as other glyphs have been found in the Dan River in Stokes County

Figure 7.16. Cranberry Rock, Ashe County, North Carolina.

(Espenshade 2012) and the Hiwassee River in Clay and Jackson counties, and along trails, on mountaintops, and in rockshelters in western North Carolina and northwestern Georgia. Loubser et al. (2019:200) suggest that "the specific placement and contents of these petroglyphs show that they occupy a space where visible physical and invisible spiritual realms overlap." Two of the better-known petroglyph sites in southwestern North Carolina are Hiwassee Rock in Clay County and Judaculla Rock in Jackson County. Hiwassee Rock is a large slate boulder on the bank of Hiwassee River. Carved into its surface are clockwise spirals, cupules, serpentine forms, and a legged creature with a long tail (Loubser et al. 2019). This is one of a series of carved rocks and boulders along a 5 km stretch of Hiwassee River. Judaculla Rock is a large boulder of soapstone in which were carved approximately 1,548 glyphs, most of which are cupules (Wilburn 1952). These rocks and their symbols undoubtedly held powerful cosmological meaning for the Cherokees and their ancestors.

8

Contact: Late May 1540 CE

Word of the bearded white men wielding thunder sticks that kill from a distance, brandishing long, sharp reflective blades, and riding giant animals that look like elk but have no antlers, spread from village to village like the wind. The chief of Joara thought he was prepared. He had heard that the white warriors traveled with some of their own food—grunting dog-like animals with flat snouts, but that they also demanded a lot of maize. Despite the cooler weather, his people had been able to store much maize and some beans from the previous year's harvest. They also had many pots of passenger pigeon oil. And the fish were still spawning in the river next to their village. He had also heard that the white men liked dog meat. There were plenty of dogs.

He gathered his people together in the plaza in front of his house, which stood on a low mound. From this dais he spoke of the impending arrival of the monster—an army of white men that sat on giant beasts, and how he and his people would welcome and feed the monster in the hope that they would gain much in return. He asked his people to prepare by hiding reserves of dried maize for themselves and to prepare baskets of maize for their guests. He asked them to be generous with their possessions such as pearls, baskets, dogs, and slaves. And he promised that he would share with them anything of value that he might obtain from the white men. He concluded by telling them that he and his people might gain great power and status through this encounter, if it went well, or that they might be destroyed if it did not.

The next morning his two scouts reported that the monster would arrive before sunset. By mid-afternoon crows flew overhead squawking a warning. Other birds soon followed suit. Then the people heard a noise like thousands of rocks falling down a hill, drowning out the sounds of the river and the birds. The pathway that led along the river into their village was wide enough for only two or three to emerge at a time. The men and their mounts spilled from the edge of the woods, their armor and swords reflecting the sunlight and their giant wolf dogs barking at the petrified villagers. The leader of the white men preceded the rest, and by his side was a man of a familiar and friendly tribe known to reside to the south and who spoke the same language as the chief.

Standing tall and with outstretched arms and fingers, the chief welcomed his guests at the edge of the village. The men, women and children behind him silently quaked in fear at the spectacle before them, as soldiers, horses, dogs, and pigs continued to thunder from the woods, seemingly without end. Awkward greetings were exchanged and the chief indicated, mostly with gestures, that the white men were welcome in his village and that his people would attend to their needs. Ultimately, with some difficulty it was communicated that the white men were interested only in finding bright yellow, heavy rocks. The white leader held a small, flattened disk of one in his hand to indicate his quest. The chief had never seen this rock before but, observing its similarity to copper, offered the white leader some copper beads he had won by exchange with a chief in the mountains. The white leader shook his head to indicate that this was not what he was seeking, but seemed intrigued and wished to know where the copper rock could be found. He knew that gold would more likely turn up in the rock formations of mountains. Through the interpreter, who had learned a few words of the white men, the chief indicated that there was copper in the mountains to the northwest, and that the people who lived there knew where to find it.

After five days they left. The chief looked out from his house on the small mound overlooking his village and wondered at the devastation wrought by his visitors. The white men's beasts had trampled the newly planted fields of maize. Nearly all of their food was gone. Most of their slaves and dogs were gone. He went back into his house, smoked some tobacco, closed his eyes and traveled in his mind to the future. What he saw was a pair of vultures circling in a gray, stormy sky above a ground on which everything was dead.

******

The Appalachian Summit was in the midst of the Little Ice Age when Hernando de Soto passed through on May 25, 1540. Indeed, Rodrigo Angel, a private secretary to de Soto, wrote:

> Tuesday, on the twenty-fifth of May, they left from Xuala and crossed that day a very high mountain range, and they spent the night in a small forest, and the next

8. Contact: Late May 1540 CE

day, Wednesday, in a savannah where they endured great cold, although it was already the twenty-sixth of May; and there they crossed, in water up to their shins, the river by which they afterward left in the brigantines that they made [Clayton et al. 1993:281].

Xuala, later referred to as "Joara," is known to archaeologists as the Berry site, located along Upper Creek, a tributary of the Catawba River in Burke County, North Carolina. When de Soto and his massive entrada passed through the mountains on their way from Joara to Guasili, located west of the Blue Ridge, they encountered no humans. The route that they took through the mountains is contested (Beck 1997; Boyd and Schroedl 1987; Hudson et al. 1984; Sampeck et al. 2015; Swanton 1985), but most recent analyses and archaeological evidence puts the mountain crossing through Elk Park in Avery County, North Carolina (Figure 8.1) (Sampeck et al. 2015). Although they encountered no humans in their mountain crossing, the impact that de Soto and his successors had on native peoples and the cultural landscape of the larger

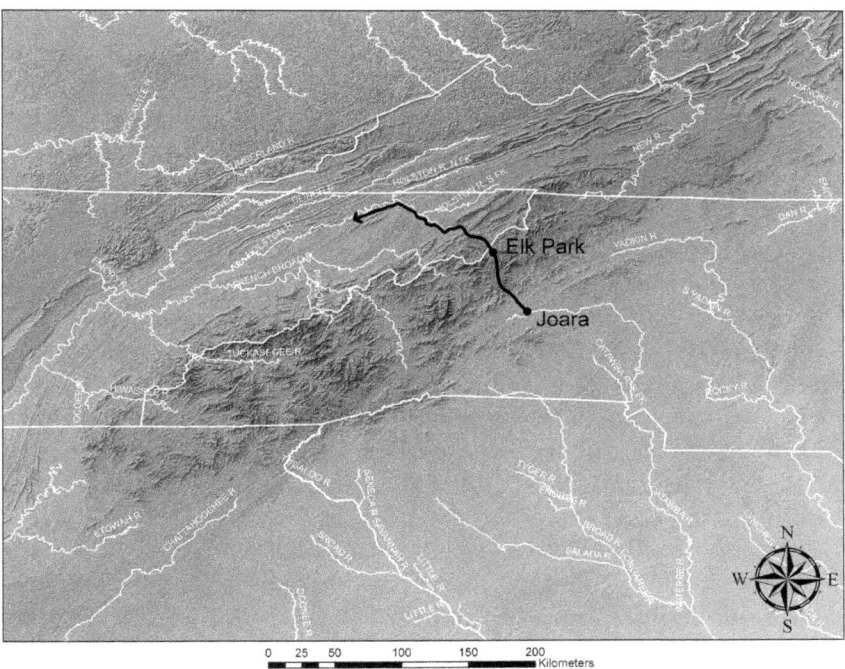

Figure 8.1. Proposed route of Hernando de Soto through western North Carolina (from Sampeck et al. 2015).

Boone Before Boone

Southeast was devastating. The Spaniards arrived at a time when indigenous populations were already vulnerable due to the Little Ice Age that lasted from 1400 to 1850 CE. They also arrived in spring when stores of maize from the previous harvest would have been all but exhausted. Indeed, a Portuguese member of the entrada known only as the "Gentleman from Elvas" reported that when they arrived in Guaxulle (Guasili):

> The Indians there made him service of three hundred dogs, for they observed that the Christians liked them and sought them to eat; but they are not eaten among them (the Indians). In Guaxulle and along that road there was very little maize.
> The governor (de Soto) sent an Indian thense with a message to the cacique of Chiaha, asking him to order some maize brought them, so that they might rest several days in Chiaha [Clayton et al. 1993:87].

Along their path to the Mississippi the Spaniards evidently consumed much of the food of every village they visited, captured or were given many people for use as guides, translators, and insurance for safe travel, slaughtered hundreds of natives, and may have introduced viruses to which the natives had no resistance.

The next known European visitor to the region was Captain Juan Pardo, who established a garrison, Fort San Juan, manned with 30 men at Joara in 1567. Archaeologists have excavated a part of this fort and its associated structures, finding several 16th-century Spanish artifacts (Beck et al. 2006). In summer 1567, the garrison's Sergeant Moyano, 20 soldiers, and a group of native warriors set out northwest through the mountains to exact revenge on the chiefs of two villages, one of which may have been near present-day Saltville, Virginia (Beck 1997). In the following September, Juan Pardo crossed through the mountains to rescue Moyano and his men who were reported held captive in Chiaha. According to Pardo, he "passed the mountains in four days of uninhabited areas" (Pardo 1990:314). In November, after returning to Fort San Juan, Pardo departed, again leaving 30 men at the fort. Less than a year later it was reported that the Indians had attacked and killed all of the Spaniards. Thus ended Spain's foothold in interior North Carolina.

Nearly one hundred years later English colonists explored the Southern Appalachian Mountains and beyond, beginning with the journey of Thomas Batts and Robert Fallam in 1671. Their path led them from Fort Henry in eastern Virginia across the Blue Ridge and into southern West Virginia by way of the New River (Shefveland 2016). Three years later, James Needham and Gabriel Arthur set out from Fort Henry to establish trading alliances with the Cherokee

8. Contact: Late May 1540 CE

(Davis 1990). Their path took a more southerly route, likely following the Yadkin River into the Mountains. In December 1751, the Moravian Bishop, August Gottlieb Spangenberg probably came very close to Boone in his survey of lands for a Moravian mission (Arthur 1915). Like the Spanish and English explorers before him, he encountered no native human life in the high mountain valleys. And then came Daniel Boone.

Archaeological Evidence

In support of this historical evidence of a vacant quarter in the northwestern mountains of North Carolina, there is very little archaeological evidence of a native presence after 1350 CE, when the winters and short growing seasons of the Little Ice Age began to take their toll. Artifacts that would readily identify native activity in the region between 1350 and 1769 CE (when Daniel Boone arrived) include Qualla phase pottery associated with the Cherokee of southwestern North Carolina, and Burke phase pottery possibly associated with Siouan speakers such as those who occupied the Berry site in Burke County, North Carolina. No Qualla pottery has been found in the northwestern counties of the state; its distribution corresponds with the Valley, Out, and Middle Cherokee towns of southwestern North Carolina. Burke pottery, found primarily in the eastern foothills of the Blue Ridge at the headwaters of the Yadkin and Catawba, has been found in trace amounts on sites in the Watauga River valley (Figure 7.15). This suggests some seasonal use or transhumance, but not permanent residence in the region during the Little Ice Age. It is likely that the gaps and river valleys that connected the eastern foothills of the Blue Ridge with the VRP west of the Blue Ridge facilitated human travel and interaction between those regions throughout the human past. This may explain remarkable similarity between the material culture (especially pottery) of the Burke phase in North Carolina and the contemporaneous Nolichucky phase on the other side of the mountains in northeastern Tennessee (Whyte and Boyd 2019). In contrast, northward travels of Qualla phase people would likely have followed pathways through the lowlands of the northeastward-trending VRP or through the rolling hills of the Piedmont Plateau to the east. In other words, the commonly held belief that northwestern North Carolina was *inhabited* by the Cherokee (Arthur 1915:15) is likely a myth.

Boone Before Boone

Summary

The native occupation of northwestern North Carolina essentially ended with the onset of the Little Ice Age between 1350 and 1400 CE. European explorers of the region encountered people living in villages on either side of the northern mountains but not within. Records of their travels emphasize the harsh temperatures and terrain of the region, especially regarding the needs of their horses. The scant archaeological evidence of native peoples visiting the uplands during the Little Ice Age and coinciding with European encounters in adjacent regions indicates connections with the upper Catawba and Yadkin River valleys that were most likely occupied by Siouan speaking groups, some of which may have been ancestors of today's Catawbas. Euro-American colonists encountered no native resistance to their land claims. When Benjamin Ward built his cabin on a terrace where Watauga River and Cove Creek come together in Western Watauga County, he probably noticed the many artifacts in his fields, but doubtfully realized that he was living on one of the last of the native villages of the region.

Conclusion

It may surprise many readers that the Appalachian Summit region has experienced such a rich human presence for nearly fourteen thousand years. For most of that time small groups of people, like today's southern tourists and second-home owners, visited the uplands only seasonally, albeit foraging and hunting for the many and varied food resources that abound especially in summer and fall. It was not until a few hundred years prior to European contact that native people of the Appalachian Summit settled into village life. They left no written record, yet we have learned much of their existence from archaeology—the scientific study of things they left behind. One only has to reflect on the past fourteen thousand years of European, Asian, or African history to realize the cultural and linguistic variation that must have existed within that vast block of time. In addition to the material evidence of technologies, structures, etcetera that are readily expressed in the archaeological record, there must have been many languages, cosmologies, and customs that have left little or no trace.

It also is enlightening, for perspective, to compare historical events of other continents to those of the Appalachian region. While humans were beginning to explore the Appalachian Summit in the Middle Paleoindian period, Ice Age peoples were creating the beautiful Upper Paleolithic paintings in Altamira Cave in northern Spain. When Early Archaic people were camped out at the Dutch Creek site near Valle Crucis nine thousand years ago, villagers in what is now Iraq were starting to cultivate barley and wheat for making gruel and beer. In the Middle Archaic period, seven thousand years ago, when hunters and gatherers were eating porcupines in Church Rockshelter No. 1, ancient Chinese people were cultivating millet and rice, making elaborate pottery, and had begun to develop a written record that included individual characters for various gods, the sun, and the moon. While Late Archaic period natives of the Appalachian region were making

Conclusion

cooking vessels of soapstone, nearly four thousand years ago, the powerful Egyptian pharaoh Hatshepsut built her remarkable funerary temple in western Thebes and ancient Celts had begun to construct Stonehenge in Whitshire, England. In the Late Woodland period, at approximately 1000 CE, when the first villages began to appear in the higher valleys of the Appalachian Summit, the Norse had made landfall in the "New World" and built a settlement, L'Anse aux Meadows, on the island of Newfoundland. More Europeans, with a profound and lasting impact, were soon to come.

Bibliography

Adovasio, J. M., and D. Pedler. 2016. *Strangers in a New Land: What Archaeology Reveals About the First Americans.* Buffalo, New York: Firefly Books.

Adovasio, J. M., J. D. Gunn, J. Donahue, and R. Stuckenrath. 1978. Meadowcroft Rockshelter, 1977: An Overview. *American Antiquity* 43:632–651.

Aldhouse-Green, M. 2015. *Bog Bodies Uncovered: Solving Europe's Ancient Mystery.* New York: Thames & Hudson.

Anderson, D. G., and G. T. Hanson. 1988. Early Archaic Settlement in the Southeastern United States: A Case Study from the Savannah River Valley. *American Antiquity* 53:262–286.

Anderson, D. G., and K. E. Sassaman. 1996. Paleoindian and Early Archaic Research in the South Carolina Area. In *The Paleoindian and Early Archaic Southeast,* edited by D. G. Anderson and K. E. Sassaman, pp. 222–237. Tuscaloosa: University of Alabama Press.

Applegate, D. 2013. The Early-Middle Woodland Landscape in Kentucky. In *Early and Middle Woodland Landscapes of the Southeast,* edited by A. P. Wright and E. R. Henry, pp. 19–44. Gainesville: University Presses of Florida.

Arthur, J. P. 1915. *A History of Watauga County, North Carolina.* Richmond: Everett Waddey.

Ashcraft, S., C. Espenshade, and J. Loubser. 2012. Hiwassee River Petroglyphs. Paper presented at the 77th annual meeting of the Society for American Archaeology, Memphis, Tennessee.

Bass, Q. R. 1977. Prehistoric Settlement and Subsistence Patterns in the Great Smoky Mountains. Unpublished M.A. thesis, Department of Anthropology, University of Tennessee, Knoxville.

Beck, R. A., Jr. 1997. From Joara to Chiaha: Spanish Exploration of the Appalachian Summit Area, 1540–1568. *Southeastern Archaeology* 16:162–169.

Beck, R. A., Jr., D. G. Moore, and C. B. Rodning. 2006. Identifying Fort San Juan: A Sixteenth-Century Spanish Occupation at the Berry Site, North Carolina. *Southeastern Archaeology* 25:65–77.

Bourgeon, L., A. Burke, and T. Higham. 2017. Earliest Human Presence in North America Dated to the Last Glacial Maximum: New Radiocarbon Dates from Bluefish Caves, Canada. PLoS One: http://doi.org/10.1371/journal.pone.0169486.

Boyd, C. C., Jr. 1986. *Archaeological Investigations in the Watauga Reservoir, Carter and Johnson Counties, Tennessee.* Knoxville: University of Tennessee Department of Anthropology Report of Investigations No. 44.

———. 1987. The 1986 Test Excavations at the Plum Grove Site (40WG17), Washington County, Tennessee. In *Upland Archaeology in the East: A Third Symposium,* edited by M. B. Barber, pp. 282–299. Atlanta: Cultural Resources Report No. 87–1, U.S. Forest Service, Southern Region.

Bibliography

Boyd, C. C., Jr., and G. F. Schroedl. 1987. In Search of Coosa. *American Antiquity* 52:840–844.

Bradbury, A. P. 1997 The Bow and Arrow in the Eastern Woodlands: Evidence for an Archaic Origin. *North American Archaeologist* 18:207–233.

Brinton, D. G. 1901. *The American Race: A Linguistic Classification and Ethnographic Description of the Native Tribes of North and South America.* Philadelphia: David McKay.

Broyles, B. J. 1966. Preliminary Report: The St. Albans Site (46Ka27), Kanawha County, West Virginia. *The West Virginia Archaeologist* 19:1–43.

_____. 1971. Second Preliminary Report: The St. Albans Site (46Ka27), Kanawha County, West Virginia, 1964–1968. Report of Archaeological Investigations, No. 3. Morgantown: West Virginia Geological and Economic Survey.

Caldwell, J. R. 1964. Interaction Spheres in Prehistory. In *Hopewellian Studies*, edited by J. R. Caldwell and R. L. Hall, pp. 133–143. Springfield: Illinois State Museum.

Chapman, J. 1975. *The Rose Island Site and the Bifurcate Point Tradition.* University of Tennessee, Department of Anthropology, Report of Investigations 14, Knoxville.

_____. 1977. *Archaic Period Research in the Lower Little Tennessee River Valley—1975, Icehouse Bottom, Harrison Branch, Thirty Acre Island, Calloway Island.* Department of Anthropology, University of Tennessee, Reports of Investigations 18, Knoxville.

_____. 1978. *The Bacon Farm Site and a Buried Site Reconnaissance.* Department of Anthropology, University of Tennessee, Reports of Investigations 21, Knoxville.

_____. 1979. *The Howard and Calloway Island Sites.* Department of Anthropology, University of Tennessee, Reports of Investigations 23, Knoxville.

_____. 1981. *The Bacon Bend and Iddins Sites: The Late Archaic Period in the Lower Little Tennessee River Valley.* University of Tennessee, Department of Anthropology, Report of Investigations 31, Knoxville.

_____. 1990. *The Kimberly-Clark Site and Site 40LD207.* Tennessee Anthropological Association Miscellaneous Paper 14.

Chapman, J., and A. B. Shea. 1981. The Archaeobotanical Record: Early Archaic to Contact in the Lower Little Tennessee River Valley. *Tennessee Anthropologist* 6:61–84.

Chapman, J., and B. C. Keel. 1979. Candy Creek–Connestee Components in Eastern Tennessee and Western North Carolina and their Relationship with Adena-Hopewell. In *Hopewell Archaeology*, edited by D. S. Brose and N. Greber, pp. 157–161. Kent, Ohio: Kent State University Press.

Claassen, C., and M. E. Compton. 2012. Rock Features of Western North Carolina. In *The Archaeology of North Carolina: Three Archaeological Symposia*, edited by C. R. Ewen, T. R. Whyte, and R. P. S. Davis, Jr. North Carolina Archaeological Council Publication No. 30, Raleigh.

Clark, J. 1993. *Unexplained! 347 Strange Sightings, Incredible Occurrences, and Puzzling Physical Phenomena.* Canton, Michigan: Visible Ink Press.

Clayton, L. A., V. J. Knight, Jr., and E. C. Moore (eds). 1993. *The De Soto Chronicles: The Expedition of Hernando De Soto to North America in 1539–1543*, Volume I. Tuscaloosa: University of Alabama Press.

Coe, J. L. 1964. *The Formative Cultures of the Carolina Piedmont.* Transactions of the American Philosophical Society, n.s., 54(5). Philadelphia, Pennsylvania.

Coe, J. L., and E. Lewis. 1952. Dan River Series Statement. In *Prehistoric Pottery of the Eastern United States*, edited by J. B. Griffin. Ann Arbor: Museum of Anthropology, University of Michigan.

Collins, S. M. 1977. *A Prehistoric Community at the Macon County Industrial Park Site.* North Carolina Archaeological Council Publication 2, Raleigh.

Bibliography

Crites, G. D. 1998. 31MD60 and 31MD280 Archaeobotanical Remains. In *Data Recovery at Prehistoric Site 31MD60, Madison County, North Carolina*, edited by S. Shumate, L. Kimball, and P. Evans-Shumate, pp. 10.4–10.14. Appalachian State University Laboratories of Archaeological Science. Submitted to the North Carolina Department of Transportation, Raleigh.

Davis, R. P. S., Jr. (ed). 1990. The Travels of James Needham and Gabriel Arthur through Virginia, North Carolina, and Beyond, 1673–1674. *Southern Indian Studies* 39:31–55.

Delcourt, P. A., and H. R. Delcourt. 1980. Vegetation Maps for Eastern North America: 40,000 Yr B.P. to the Present. In *Geobotany II*, edited by R. C. Romans, pp. 123–165. New York: Plenum.

_____, and _____. 1997. Pre-Columbian Native American Use of Fire on Southern Appalachian Landscapes. *Conservation Biology* 11:1010–1014.

Delcourt, P. A., H. R. Delcourt, C. R. Ison, W. E. Sharp, and K. J. Gremillion. 1998. Prehistoric Human Use of Fire, the Eastern Agricultural Complex, and Appalachian Oak-Chestnut Forests: Paleoecology of Cliff Palace Pond, Kentucky. *American Antiquity* 63:263–278.

Dickens, R S, Jr. n.d. Preliminary Report on Archaeological Investigations at the Plum Grove Site (40WG17), Washington County, Tennessee. Ms. On file, Department of Anthropology, Georgia State University, Atlanta.

_____. 1976. *Cherokee Prehistory: The Pisgah Phase in the Appalachian Summit Region*. Knoxville: University of Tennessee Press.

Dillehay, T. D. 1989. *Monte Verde, a Late Pleistocene Settlement in Chile*. Washington, D.C.: Smithsonian Institution Press.

Discover. 1994. The Mummies of Xinjiang. *Discover*, April 1, 1994.

Driskell, B. N. 1996. Stratified Late Pleistocene and Early Holocene Deposits at Dust Cave, Northwestern Alabama. In *The Paleoindian and Early Archaic Southeast*, pp. 315–330, edited by D. G. Anderson and K. E. Sassaman. Tuscaloosa: University of Alabama Press.

Dunbar, J. S., and S. D. Webb. 1996. Bone and Ivory Tools from Submerged Paleoindian Sites in Florida. In *The Paleoindian and Early Archaic Southeast*, pp. 331–353, edited by D. G. Anderson and K. E. Sassaman. Tuscaloosa: University of Alabama Press.

Espenshade, C.T. 2012. Indian Rock on the Dan River. *North Carolina Archaeology* 61:122–127.

Evans, C. 1955. *A Ceramic Study of Virginia Archaeology*. Bureau of American Ethnology, Bulletin 160. Washington, D.C.: Smithsonian Institution.

Fagan, B. 2008. *The Great Warming: Climate Change and the Rise and Fall of Civilizations*. New York: Bloomsbury.

Fiegel, K. H., B. J. McGraw, and J. L. Hixon. 1992. Archaeological Investigation of the Kay Shelter in Beathitt County, Kentucky. In *Current Archaeological Research in Kentucky*, Volume 2, edited by D. Pollack and A. G. Henderson, pp 43–54. Kentucky Heritage Council, Frankfort, Kentucky.

Fleckinger, A. 2018. *Ötzi, the Iceman: The Full Facts at a Glance*. Vienna: Bolzano.

GAI Consultants, Inc. 1986. *Phase III Data Recovery Investigation at the Stratton Meadows Site (31GH98) on the Tellico Plains-Robbinsville Highway, Graham County, North Carolina and Monroe County, Tennessee*. Submitted to the Federal Highway Administration, Arlington, Virginia.

Gardner, W. M. 1977. Flint Run Paleoindian Complex and Its Implications for Eastern North American Prehistory. In *Amerinds and their Paleoenvironments in Eastern*

Bibliography

North America, pp. 257–263, edited by W. S. Newman and B. Salwen. The New York Academy of Sciences, volume 288.

———. 1983. Get Me to the Quarry on Time: The Flint Run Paleoindian Complex Revisited (Again). Paper presented at the 48th annual meeting of the Society for American Archaeology, Pittsburgh.

———. 1989. An Examination of Culture Change in the Late Pleistocene and Early Holocene (circa 9200 to 6800 B.C.). In *Paleoindian Research in Virginia: A Synthesis*, edited by J. M. Wittkofski and T. R. Reinhart, pp. 5–52. Special Publication No. 19 of the Archeological Society of Virginia, Richmond.

Goldman-Finn, N. S., and R. B. Walker. 1994. The Dust Cave Bone Tool Assemblage. *Journal of Alabama Archaeology* 40 (1&2):107–115.

Goodyear, A. C., K. E. Sassaman, N. Powell, T. Charles, and C. B. DePratter. 1990. An Unusually Large Biface from the Phil Neeley Site, 38BM85, Bamberg County, South Carolina. *South Carolina Antiquities* 22:1–15.

Gremillion, K. J. 1996. The Paleoethnobotanical Record for the Mid-Holocene Southeast. In *Archaeology of the Mid-Holocene Southeast*, edited by K. E. Sassaman and D. G. Anderson, pp. 99–114. Gainesville: University Press of Florida.

Guilday, J. E., P. W. Parmalee, and H. W. Hamilton. 1977. *The Clark's Cave Bone Deposit and the Late Pleistocene Paleoecology of the Central Appalachian Mountains of Virginia*. Bulletin of the Carnegie Museum of Natural History No. 2, Pittsburgh.

Halligan, J. J., M. R. Waters, A. Perrotti, I. J. Jones, J. M. Feingerg, and M. D. Bourne. 2016. Pre-Clovis Occupation 14,550 Years Ago at the Page-Ladson Site, Florida, and the Peopling of the Americas. *Science Advances* 2, no. 5, e11600375. DOI: 10.1126/sciadv.1600375.

Heizer, R. F., and L. K. Napton. 1970. *Archaeology and the Prehistoric Great Basin Lacustrine Subsistence Regine as Seen from Lovelock Cave, Nevada*. Contributions to the University of California Archaeological Research Facility 10.

Hildebrandt, W. R., and K. R. McGuire. 2002. The Ascendance of Hunting during the California Middle Archaic: An Evolutionary Perspective. *American Antiquity* 67:231–256.

Holden, P. P. 1966. An Archaeological Survey of Transylvania County, North Carolina. Unpublished M.A. thesis, University of North Carolina, Chapel Hill.

Homsey, L. K., and S. C. Sherwood. 2010. Interpretation of Prepared Clay Surfaces at Dust Cave, Alabama: The Role of Actualistic Studies. *Ethnoarchaeology* 2(1):73–98.

Homsey, L. K., R. B. Walker, and K. D. Hollenbach. 2010. What's for Dinner? Investigating Food-Processing Technologies at Dust Cave, Alabama. *Southeastern Archaeology* 29:182–196.

Hudson, C. 1976. *The Southeastern Indians*. Knoxville: University of Tennessee Press.

Hudson, C., M. Smith, and C. DePratter. 1984. The Hernando de Soto Expedition: From Apalachee to Chiaha. *Southeastern Archaeology* 3:65–77.

Jefferies, R. W. 1996 The Emergence of Long-Distance Exchange Networks in the Southeastern United States. In *Archaeology of the Mid-Holocene Southeast*, edited by K. E. Sassaman and D. G. Anderson, pp. 222–234. Gainesville: University Press of Florida.

Johnson, M. F. 1996. Paleoindians Near the Edge: A Virginia Perspective. In *The Paleoindian and Early Archaic Southeast*, pp. 187–212, edited by D. G. Anderson and K. E. Sassaman. Tuscaloosa: University of Alabama Press.

Keel, B. C. 1976. *Cherokee Archaeology: A Study of the Appalachian Summit*. Knoxville: University of Tennessee Press.

Bibliography

Keeler, R. W. 1971. An Archaeological Survey of the Upper Catawba River Valley. Unpublished B.A. thesis, Department of Anthropology, University of North Carolina, Chapel Hill.
Kelly, L. A. 2003. The Context of the Post Pit and Meaning of the Sacred Pole at the East St. Louis Mound Group. *Wisconsin Archaeologist* 84:107–125.
Kennedy, D., and M. C. Bishop. 2011. Google Earth and the Archaeology of Saudi Arabia: A Case Study from the Jeddah Area. *Journal of Archaeological Science* 38:1284–1293.
Kerber, J. 1997. Native American Treatment of Dogs in Northeastern North America: Archaeological and Ethnohistorical Perspectives. *Archaeology of Eastern North America* 25:81–96.
Kimball, L. R. 1985. The 1977 Archaeological Survey: An Overall Assessment of the Archaeological Resources of Tellico Reservoir. University of Tennessee, Department of Anthropology, Report of Investigations 40, Knoxville.
_____. 1994. Microwear Analysis of Archaic and Early Woodland Tools from the Main Site (15BL35), Kentucky. In *Upper Cumberland Archaic and Woodland Period Archaeology at the Main Site (15BL35), Bell County, Kentucky,* Appendix F, by S. D. Creasman. Lexington, Kentucky: Cultural Resource Analysts, Inc.
_____. 1996. Early Archaic Settlement and Technology: Lessons from Tellico. In *The Paleoindian and Early Archaic Southeast,* pp. 149–186, edited by D. G. Anderson and K. E. Sassaman. Tuscaloosa: University of Alabama Press.
_____. 2019. War Points? In *Archaeological Adaptation,* edited by C. C. Boyd, Jr., pp. 19–46. University of Tennessee Press, Knoxville.
Kimball, L. R., and J. Wolf. 2017. The Ritualized Landscape at Biltmore Mound. *North Carolina Archaeology* 66:39–73.
Kimball, L. R., and T. R. Whyte. 1992. An Archaeological Survey of Lots 16 and 17 on Winklers Meadow Road, Boone, North Carolina. Submitted to the North Carolina Office of State Archaeology, Raleigh.
Kimball, L. R., T. R. Whyte, and G. D. Crites. 2010. The Biltmore Mound and Hopewellian Mound Use in the Southern Appalachians. *Southeastern Archaeology* 29:44–58.
Kjaer, K. H., N. K. Larsen, T. Biinder, A. A. Bjørk, O. Eisen, M. A. Fahnestock, S. Funder, A. A. Garde, H. Haack, V. Helm, M. Houmark-Nielsen, K. K. Kjeldsen, S. A. Khan, H. Machguth, I. McDonald, M. Morlighem, J. Mouginot, J. D. Paden, T. E. Waight, C. Weikusat, E. Willerslev, and J. A. MacGregor. 2018. A Large Impact Crater beneath Hiawatha Glacier in Northwest Greenland. *Science Advances* 4:eaar8173.
Kneberg, M. 1956. Some Important Projectile Point Types Found in the Tennessee Area. *Tennessee Archaeologist* 12:17–28.
_____. 1957. Chipped Stone Artifacts of the Tennessee Valley Area. *Tennessee Archaeologist* 8:55–65.
_____. 1961. Four Southeastern Limestone-tempered Pottery Complexes. *Southeastern Archaeological Conference Newsletter* 7:3–14.
Kroeber, A. L. 1939. *Cultural and Natural Areas of Native North America.* University of California Publications in American Archaeology and Ethnology 38.
Lafferty, R. H., III. 1981. *The Phipps Bend Archaeological Project.* TVA Publications in Anthropology No. 26, Norris, Tennessee.
Lane, L., and D. G. Anderson. 2001. Paleoindian Occupations of the Southern Appalachians. In *Archaeology of the Appalachian Highlands,* edited by L. P. Sullivan and S. C. Prezzano, pp. 88–102. Knoxville: University of Tennessee Press.

Bibliography

Lankford, G.E. 2007. *Reachable Stars: Patterns in the Ethnoastronomy of Eastern North America*. Tuscaloosa: University of Alabama Press.

Ledbetter, R. J., D. G. Anderson, L. D. O'Steen, and D. T. Elliott. 1996. Paleoindian and Early Archaic Research in Georgia. In *The Paleoindian and Early Archaic Southeast*, pp. 222–237, edited by D. G. Anderson and K. E. Sassaman. Tuscaloosa: University of Alabama Press.

Lewis, T. M. N., and M. K. Lewis. 1961. *Eva: An Archaic Site*. Knoxville: The University of Tennessee Press.

Lewis, T. M. N., and M. Kneberg. 1957. The Camp Creek Site. *Tennessee Archaeologist* 8:1–48.

Loubser, Johannes, Scott Ashcraft, and James Wettstaed. 2019. Betwixt and Between: The Occurrence of Petroglyphs between Townhouses of the Living and Townhouses of Spirit Beings in Northern Georgia and Western North Carolina. In *Transforming the Landscape: Rock Art and the Mississippian Cosmos*, edited by Carol Diaz-Granados, Jan Simek, George Sabo III, and Mark Wagner, pp. 200–244. Havertown, Pennsylvania: Oxbow.

Lounsbury, F. G. 1961. Iroquois-Cherokee Linguistic Relations. In *Symposium on Cherokee and Iroquois Culture*, edited by W. N. Fenton and J. Gulick, pp. 9–17. Bureau of American Ethnology, Bulletin 180. Smithsonian Institution, Washington, D.C.

Malhi, R.S., B.A. Schultz and D.G. Smith. 2001. Distribution of Mitochondrial DNA Lineages Among Native American Tribes of Eastern North America. *Human Biology* 73:17–55.

Manzano, B. L. 1985. Faunal Resources, Butchering Patterns, and Seasonality at the Eastman Rockshelter (40SL34): An Interpretation of Function. Unpublished M.A. thesis, University of Tennessee, Knoxville.

Marcoux, J. B. 2012. Glass Trade Beads from the English Colonial Period in the Southeast, ca. A.D. 1607–1783. *Southeastern Archaeology* 31:157–184.

Martin, P. S. 1967. Pleistocene Overkill. In *Pleistocene Extinctions: The Search for a Cause*, pp. 75–120, edited by P. S. Martin and H. E. Wright. New Haven, Connecticut: Yale University Press.

Mathis, M. A. 1982. The Blue Rock Soapstone Quarry (31Yc7), Yancey County, North Carolina. In *Collected Papers on the Archaeology of North Carolina*, pp. 82–103, edited by J. B. Mountjoy. North Carolina Archaeological Council Publication No. 19.

McAvoy, J. M., and L. D. McAvoy. 2015. *Nottoway River Survey Part II: Cactus Hill and Other Excavated Sites*. Nottoway River Survey Research Report No. 5. Petersburg, Virginia: Dietz Press.

McDonald, J. N. 2000. An Outline of the Pre-Clovis Archeology of SV-2, Saltville, Virginia, with Special Attention to a Bone Tool Dated 14,510 yr BP. *Jeffersonia* 9:1–60.

McLaren, D., D. Fedje, A. Dyck, Q. Mackie, A. Gauvreau, and J. Cohen. 2018. Terminal Pleistocene Epoch Human Footprints from the Pacific Coast of Canada. PLoS One: http://doi.org/10.1371/journal.pone.0193522.

Moore, C.R., A. West, M. A. LeCompte, M. J. Brooks, I. R. Daniel, Jr., A. C. Goodyear, T. A. Ferguson, A. H. Ivester, J. K. Feathers, J. P. Kennett, K. B. Tankersley, A. V. Adedeji, and T.E. Bunch. 2017. Widespread Platinum Anomaly Documented at the Younger Dryas Onset in North American Sedimentary Sequences. *Scientific Reports* 7:44031, www.nature.com/scientificreports.

Moore, D.G. 1999. Late Prehistoric and Early Historic Period Aboriginal Settlement in the Catawba Valley, North Carolina. Unpublished Ph.D. dissertation, Department of Anthropology, University of North Carolina, Chapel Hill.

Bibliography

Morgan, L.H. 1962. *League of the Iroquois.* Secaucus, New Jersey: Citadel.
Osborn, A. J. 2014. Eye of the Needle: Cold Stress, Clothing, and Sewing Technology During the Younger Dryas Cold Event in North America. *American Antiquity* 79:45–68.
Pardo, J. 1990. Relation. Translated by P. Hoffman. In *The Juan Pardo Expeditions: Explorations of the Carolinas and Tennessee, 1566–1568*, by C. Hudson. Washington, D.C.: Smithsonian Institution Press.
Perkins, P. H. 1973. North Carolina Fluted Projectile Points—Survey Report Number Two. *Southern Indian Studies* 25:3–60.
Purrington, B. L. 1975. *A Preliminary Report of Archaeological Surveys in Watauga County, North Carolina, 1970–1974.* Submitted to the North Carolina Department of Cultural Resources, Raleigh.
_____. 1983. Ancient Mountaineers: An Overview of the Prehistoric Archaeology of North Carolina's Western Mountain Region. In *The Prehistory of North Carolina: An Archaeological Symposium*, pp. 83–160, edited by M. A. Mathis and J. J. Crow. Raleigh: North Carolina Division of Archives and History, Department of Cultural Resources.
Redmond, B. G., and K. B. Tankersley. 2005. Evidence of Early Paleoindian Bone Modification and Use at the Sheriden Cave Site (33wy252), Wyandot County, Ohio. *American Antiquity* 70:503–526.
Riggs, B. H. 1985. Dated Contexts from Watauga Reservoir: Cultural Chronology Building for Northeast Tennessee. In *Exploring Tennessee Prehistory: A Dedication to Alfred K. Guthe*, edited by T. R. Whyte, C. C. Boyd, Jr., and B. H. Riggs, pp.169–184. University of Tennessee, Department of Anthropology, Report of Investigations No. 42, Knoxville.
_____. 2012. *Uk'tena* Lives Here. Paper presented at the 69th annual meeting of the Southeastern Archaeological Conference, Baton Rouge, Louisiana.
Rindos, D. 1980. Symbiosis, Instability, and the Origins and Spread of Agriculture: A New Model. *Current Anthropology* 21:751–772.
Ritchie, W. A. 1932. *The Lamoka Site: The Type Station of the Archaic Algonkin Period in New York.* New York State Archaeological Association, Research Transactions 7(4). Rochester, New York.
_____. 1940. *Two Prehistoric Village Sites at Brewerton, New York.* Rochester Museum of Arts and Sciences, Research Records No. 5. Rochester, New York.
Rodning, C. B. 2008. Temporal Variation in Qualla Pottery at Coweeta Creek. *North Carolina Archaeology* 57:1–49.
Runquist, Jeannette. 1979. Analysis of the Flora and Faunal Remains from Proto-Historic North Carolina Cherokee Indian Sites. Ph.D. dissertation, Department of Zoology, North Carolina State University, Raleigh.
Sampeck, K., J. Thayn, and H. H. Earnest, Jr. 2015. Geographic Information System Modeling of De Soto's Route from Joara to Chiaha: Archaeology and Anthropology of Southeastern Road Networks in the Sixteenth Century. *American Antiquity* 80:46–66.
Sassaman, K. E. 2001 Articulating Hidden Histories of the Mid-Holocene in the Southern Appalachians. In *Archaeology of the Appalachian Highlands*, edited by L. P. Sullivan and S. C. Prezanno, pp. 103–120. Knoxville: University of Tennessee Press.
Schubert, A. 2017. Mississippianization in Late Pisgah Communities in the Appalachian Summit of North Carolina. Paper presented at the 82nd annual meeting of the Society for American Archaeology, Vancouver, B.C.

Bibliography

Schuldenrein, J. 1996. Geoarchaeology and the Mid-Holocene Landscape History of the Greater Southeast. In *Archaeology of the Mid-Holocene Southeast,* edited by K. E. Sassaman and D. G. Anderson, pp. 3–27. Gainesville: University Press of Florida.

Schwarze, Edmund. 1923. *History of the Moravian Missions among Southern Indian Tribes of the United States.* Special Series No. 1, Transactions of the Moravian Historical Society. Bethlehem, Pennsylvania: Times Publishing Company.

Setzler, F. M., and J. D. Jennings. 1941. *Peachtree Mound and Village Site, Cherokee County, North Carolina.* Smithsonian Institution, Bureau of American Ethnology, Bulletin 131. Washington, D.C.

Shefveland, K. M. 2016. *Anglo-Native Virginia: Trade, Conversion, and Indian Slavery in the Old Dominion, 1646–1722.* Athens: University of Georgia Press.

Sherwood, S. C., and J. Chapman. 2005. The Identification and Potential Significance of Early Holocene Prepared Clay Surfaces: Examples from Dust Cave and Icehouse Bottom. *Southeastern Archaeology* 24:70–82.

Sherwood, S. C., B. N. Driskell, A. R. Randall, and S. C. Meeks. 2004. Chronology and Stratigraphy at Dust Cave, Alabama. *American Antiquity* 69:533–554.

Shumate, M.S. and L.R. Kimball. 2006. *Archaeological Investigations at the Coontree Picnic Area Site (31TV858) Transylvania County, North Carolina.* Appalachian State University Labs of Archaeological Science (ASU-LAS) Technical Report No. 38. Submitted to National Forests in North Carolina, Asheville.

_____, and _____. 2016. *Archaeological Investigations at the Cold Canyon Site (31SW265) Swain County, North Carolina.* Appalachian State University Labs of Archaeological Science (ASU-LAS) Technical Report No. 46. Submitted to National Forests in North Carolina, Asheville.

Siberian Times. 2013. 24,000 Year Old Boy from Lake Baikal Is "Scientific Sensation." *The Siberian Times,* October 28, 2013.

_____. 2019. 20,000-Year-Old Mammoth Murder Established: But Was It Committed by First American Migrants? *The Siberian Times,* November 13, 2019.

Speck, F. G. 1946. *Catawba Hunting, Trapping and Fishing.* Joint Publications of the Museum of the University of Pennsylvania and the Philadelphia Anthropological Society No. 2, University Museum, Philadelphia.

Stahle, D. W., M. K. Cleveland, and J. G. Hehr. 1988. North Carolina Climate Changes Reconstructed from Tree Rings: A.D. 372–1985. *Science,* New Series 240:1577–1519.

Stanford, D. J., and B. A. Bradley. 2012. *Across Atlantic Ice: The Origins of America's Clovis Culture.* Berkeley: University of California Press.

Steponaitis, V.P., J. D. Irwin, T. E. McReynolds, and C. Moore (eds.). 2006. *Stone Quarries and Sourcing in the Carolina Slate Belt.* Research Report No. 25, Research Laboratories of Archaeology, University of North Carolina at Chapel Hill.

Swanton, J. R. 1985. *Final Report of the United States De Soto Expedition Commission.* Washington, D.C.: Smithsonian Institution Press.

Thomas, C. 1985. *Report on the Mound Explorations of the Bureau of Ethnology.* Washington, D.C.: Smithsonian Institution Press.

Truncer, J. 2004. Steatite Vessel Age and Occurrence in Temperate Eastern North America. *American Antiquity* 69:487–513.

Turnbaugh, W. A. 1975 Toward an Explanation of the Broadpoint Dispersal in Eastern North American Prehistory. *Journal of Anthropological Research* 31:51–68.

Turner, E. R., III. 1989. Paleoindian Settlement Patterns and Population Distribution in Virginia. In *Paleoindian Research in Virginia: A Synthesis,* pp. 71–93, edited by

Bibliography

J. M. Wittkofski and T. R. Reinhart. Special Publication No. 19 of the Archeological Society of Virginia, Richmond.

Ulmer, Mary and Samuel E. Beck (editors). 1951. *Cherokee Cooklore: Preparing Cherokee Foods.* Cherokee, North Carolina: Mary and Goingback Chiltoskey, Stephens Press.

Versaggi, N.M., L.A.Wurst, T.C. Madrigal, and A. Lain. 2001. Adding Complexity to Late Archaic Research in the Northeastern Appalachians. In *Archaeology of the Appalachian Highlands*, pp. 121–133, edited by L. P. Sullivan and S. C. Prezzano. Knoxville: University of Tennessee Press.

Ward, H. T. 1990. The Bull in the North Carolina Buffalo. *Southern Indian Studies* 39:19–30.

Ward, H.T., and R. P. S. Davis, Jr. 1999 *Time Before History: The Archaeology of North Carolina.* Chapel Hill: University of North Carolina Press.

Webb, W. S. 1974. *Indian Knoll.* Knoxville: University of Tennessee Press.

Whyte, T. R. 1994. Archaeological Investigation of the Southwestern Portions of the Jackson Farm Site (40WG17), Unaka Ranger District, Cherokee National Forest, Tennessee. Submitted to the U.S. Forest Service, Cherokee National Forest, Cleveland, Tennessee.

_____. 1997. Lessons in Zooarchaeology from Cactus Hill, a Stratified Paleoindian through Archaic Site on the Inner Coastal Plain of Virginia. Paper presented at the Middle Atlantic Archaeological Conference, Ocean City, Maryland.

_____. 2001. Distinguishing Remains of Human Cremations from Burned Animal Bones. *Journal of Field Archaeology* 28:437–448.

_____. 2003. Prehistoric Sedentary Agriculturalists in the Appalachian Summit of Northwestern North Carolina. *North Carolina Archaeology* 52:1–19.

_____. 2005. Human Burial in the Charles Church Rockshelter, Valle Crucis, North Carolina. In *Uplands Archaeology in the East: Symposia VIII & IX*, edited by C. Nash and M. Barber, pp. 173–180. Archaeological Society of Virginia Special Publication 38–7. Richmond.

_____. 2007a. Proto-Iroquoian Divergence in the Late Archaic-Early Woodland Period Transition of the Appalachian Highlands. *Southeastern Archaeology* 26(1):134–144.

_____. 2007b. Caves versus Rockshelters: How Nomenclature Influences Interpretations of Site Function. Paper presented at the 72nd annual meeting of the Society for American Archaeology, Austin, Texas.

_____. 2010a. Archaeological Investigations at the Colvard II Site (31AH266) on the South Fork of the New River, Ashe County, North Carolina: Field Season 1. Submitted to the North Carolina Office of State Archaeology, Raleigh.

_____. 2010b. *Erethizon dorsatum* (L.) (American Porcupine) Skeletal Remains from the Charles Church Rockshelter, Watauga County, North Carolina. *Southeastern Naturalist* 9:821–826.

_____. 2011. Archaeofaunal Remains from Garden Creek Mound No. 2 (31HW2) in Haywood County, North Carolina. *North Carolina Archaeology* 60:53–64.

_____. 2013a. Dutch Creek (31WT160): A Multicomponent Prehistoric Site in Western Watauga County, North Carolina. Submitted to the North Carolina Office of State Archaeology, Raleigh.

_____. 2013b. Radiocarbon Dates on Materials and Contexts at Church Rockshelter No. 1 (31WT155), Watauga County, North Carolina. *North Carolina Archaeology* 62:1–26.

_____. 2013c. Archaeological Investigations at Church Rockshelter No. 2 (31WT39), Watauga County, North Carolina. *North Carolina Archaeology* 62:27–54.

Bibliography

———. 2014. Gifts of the Ancestors: Secondary Lithic Recycling in Appalachian Summit Prehistory. *American Antiquity* 79:679–696.

———. 2015. Prehistoric Use of Stillhouse Hollow Cave, Watauga County, North Carolina. *North Carolina Archaeology* 64:135–149.

———. 2016. Archaeofaunal Evidence of Subsistence Stress in the Middle Woodland Period at the Williams Spring Site, Madison County, Alabama. Paper presented at the 73rd annual meeting of the Southeastern Archaeological Conference, Athens, Georgia.

———. 2017a. Ceramic Vessel Manufacture in the Late Pre-Contact Period of the Appalachian Summit. *North Carolina Archaeology* 66:27–38.

———. 2017b. Household Ceramic Diversity in the Late Prehistory of the Appalachian Summit. *Southeastern Archaeology* 36:156–164.

———. 2017c. Big Meat Feasting in the Pisgah Phase of Western North Carolina. Paper presented at the 82nd annual meeting of the Society for American Archaeology, Vancouver, BC.

———. 2018a. Optically Stimulated Luminescence Dates on Early Woodland Period Pottery in Northwestern North Carolina. *North Carolina Archaeology* 76:77–86.

———. 2018b. Tiny Rockshelters and Precontact Period Ritual in Mountainous Western North Carolina. *North Carolina Archaeological Society Newsletter* 28(4):1–3.

———. 2019. An Experimental Study of Bean and Maize Burning to Interpret Evidence from Stillhouse Hollow Cave. *Southeastern Archaeology* 38:230–239.

Whyte, T. R., and C. C. Boyd, Jr. 2019. Dating the Native Plum Grove Site (40WG17), Washington County, Tennessee. In *Archaeological Adaptation*, edited by C. C. Boyd, Jr., pp. 67–82. Knoxville: University of Tennessee Press.

Whyte, T. R., and D. Johnson. 2013. Fall Harvest, Nut Processing, and the Return of the Pleiades: An Experimental Study of "Nutting Stones" in Eastern North American Archaeology. Paper presented at the 43rd Middle Atlantic Archaeological Conference, Virginia Beach, Virginia.

Whyte, T. R. and J. M. Compton. 2020. Explaining Toad Bones in Southern Appalachian Archaeological Deposits. *American Antiquity* 85:305–330.

Whyte, T. R. and L. R. Kimball. 1997. Science versus Grave Desecration: The Saga of Lake Hole Cave. *Journal of Cave and Karst Studies* 59:143–147.

———. 2017. The Birckhead Clovis Point, Watauga County, North Carolina. *North Carolina Archaeological Society Newsletter* 27(4):1–2.

Whyte, T. R., and R. S. Quick (eds). 1996. Archaeological Investigation of the Gwyn Hayes Site (31WT308) in Boone, North Carolina, Summer and Fall, 1994. Submitted to the North Carolina Department of Cultural Resources, Raleigh.

Whyte, T. R., S. A. Fleeman, and C. D. Evans. 2011. An Alternative Ontology and Experimental Study of Pottery Punctation in Southern Appalachian Region Prehistory. *Southeastern Archaeology* 30:390–398.

Wilburn, H. C. 1952. Judaculla Rock. *Southern Indian Studies* 4:19–22.

Williams, S. C. 1948 *Lieut. Henry Timberlake's Memoirs, 1756–1765*. Marietta, Georgia: Continental Books.

Winter, J. 1978. A Note on Bahamian Griddles. In *Proceedings of the Seventh International Congress for the Study of Pre-Columbian Cultures of the Lesser Antilles*, pp. 231–236. Montreal: Centre de Recherches Caraibes.

Witthoft, J. 1949. *Green Corn Ceremonialism in the Eastern Woodlands*. Occasional Contributions from the Museum of Anthropology 13. University of Michigan, Ann Arbor.

Worth, J. E. 2017. What's in a Phase? Disentangling Communities of Practice from

Bibliography

Communities of Identity in Southeastern North America. In *Forging Southeastern Identities*, edited by G. A. Waslekov and M. T. Smith, pp. 117–156. Tuscaloosa: University of Alabama Press.

Wright, A. P. 2013. Persistent Place, Shifting Practice: The Premound Landscape at the Garden Creek Site, North Carolina. In *Early and Middle Woodland Landscapes of the Southeast*, edited by A. P. Wright and E. R. Henry, pp. 108–121. Gainesville: University Press of Florida.

———. 2019. *Garden Creek: The Archaeology of Interaction in Middle Woodland Appalachia*. Tuscaloosa: University of Alabama Press.

———. 2020. *Garden Creek: The Archaeology of Interaction in Middle Woodland Appalachia*. The University of Alabama Press, Tuscaloosa.

Index

accelerator mass spectrometry 14
acorn 47, 50, 76, 80, 84, 88, 91, 94, 97, 113, 120
acorn bread/cake 47, 76, 113
Adena culture 110, 111
agriculture 130
Alligator Back formation 107
Altamira Cave, Spain 159
Altithermal Interval 58
Angel, Rodrigo 154
animal domestication 25
animal foods 25, 29, 51, 67, 96, 106, 120
animal remains 8, 12, 25, 29, 51, 67, 72, 88, 106, 107, 108, 120, 121, 122, 123, 124, 125, 139, 143, 149, 150
antler tools 18, 19, 35, 40, 48, 70, 81, 84, 102, 109, 122, 144
anvil 38, 42, 43, 47, 54, 64, 72, 89, 97, 105, 108, 139
Apalachee Indians 5
Apalchen 5
Appalachian State University (ASU) 7, 32, 34, 47, 59, 67, 69, 70, 72, 89, 104, 105, 121, 122, 136, 138, 140, 143, 144
Appalachian Stemmed knife 59, 64, 77, 78, 79, 80, 89, 90, 105, 109
Appalachian Summit (defined) 4–5
Archaeological Resources Protection Act (ARPA) 137, 143
archaeology (defined) 8; documentation 12; goals 8; history of in the Appalachian Summit 5–8; methods 10–15
architecture 77, 108, 112, 118–119, 121, 125–126, 128, 135, 137, 138, 140–141, 145, 148–150
arrow shaft 101, 106, 109–110
Arthur, Gabriel 156
Atlantic Climatic Interval 58
atlatl (spear-thrower) 44–46, 57, 60, 81, 82
atlatl weight 64–66, 81, 82
awl 48, 128, 129
axe 9, 43, 72, 77, 79, 82, 83, 92, 93, 133
axis mundi 121
Ayers, Harvard G. 7

Bacon Farm site, Tennessee 42, 43
Bahamas 46
banner stone 81
Batts, Thomas 156
beads 69, 76, 108–109, 124, 133, 137, 144, 148, 149, 154
bean 128, 129, 130. 134, 136, 153
beautiful armadillo 18, 22, 23, 144
Beringia 20, 36,
Berry site, North Carolina 146, 155, 157
bifacial thinning 45, 53, 89, 90, 105, 107
Bifurcate point tradition 40, 43, 44, 47, 49, 50, 55, 56, 60
big man 104, 120
Biltmore Mound, North Carolina 6, 116, 118, 120, 121–124, 125, 126, 140, 148
bipolar flakes/flaking 43, 45, 53, 54, 55, 105
Birckhead Clovis point 33, 34
Birckhead site, North Carolina 33–34
birdstone 102–103
bison/ buffalo 4, 17, 29
black bear 72, 93, 113, 116, 124, 125, 150
black walnut 50, 84, 88, 89, 91, 92, 94
blade 18, 25, 26, 27, 28, 32, 33, 42, 43, 45, 54, 64, 65, 113, 116, 122, 124, 125
blade core 26, 28, 116,
Blue Ridge Physiographic Province 4, 17, 35, 63, 84, 148, 155, 156, 157
Blue Rock Soapstone Quarry site 84, 92
blue-gray bedded chert 79
Bluefish Caves, Yukon 20, 36
bog mummies 9
bone needles 24, 69
bone tools 2, 18, 24, 27, 29, 31, 40, 48, 69, 70, 81, 97, 102, 108, 109, 113, 122, 123, 128, 129, 137, 144
Boone, Daniel 3, 4, 17, 157
Boone, North Carolina 2, 4, 8, 14, 29, 33, 67, 69, 70, 71, 111, 136, 157
bottle gourd 87, 92, 94, 103
bow-and-arrow 65, 81, 82, 96, 110, 111
box turtle shell rattle 112, 150
Brewerton projectile point 49, 77, 78, 89, 94, 95

Index

Brinton, D.G. 20
Brown Mountain lights 119
buffalo trails 4, 17
Bureau of American Ethnology (BAE) 5, 6, 20
burials/graves 5, 6, 11, 12, 51, 67, 69, 80, 81, 85, 86, 89, 95, 104, 107, 108, 109, 110, 121, 129, 136, 137, 138, 142–145, 149, 150
Burke pottery 146, 147, 148, 157
butternut 50, 91
Bynum Taylor site, North Carolina 80

Cactus Hill site, Virginia 15, 20, 25, 26, 29
Calvert Island, British Columbia 36
camel 29
Camp Creek projectile point 26, 101
Camp Creek site, Tennessee 81, 101, 103, 104, 106, 107–110
Candy Creek pottery 114, 115, 117
Candy Creek projectile point 101, 110
cannibalism 127
carbon-14 dating 13–14
caribou 4, 17, 22, 23, 29
carnivore gnawing 124
Catawba Indians 3, 4, 56, 158
Catawba River 3, 5, 146, 148, 155
caves 9, 12, 27, 51, 107, 112, 136, 137
celt 43, 45, 108, 109, 133, 134, 136, 139
chalcedony 26, 27, 39, 45, 52, 53, 55, 60, 61, 66, 105,106, 116, 120, 124, 125, 132, 137, 139, 144
Cherokee Indians 3, 4, 5, 6, 56, 85, 94, 95, 114, 116, 130, 134, 136, 143, 144, 145, 146, 148, 149, 152, 156, 157
Cherokee National Forest (CNF), Tennessee 136, 142–145
Cherokee Project 7
chestnut 5, 37, 38, 50, 57, 75, 76, 82, 84, 88, 93, 94, 95, 97, 120
chestnut bread/cake 47, 76, 96
Chiaha 156
Chickamauga Indians 151
chiefdom 104, 119, 132, 153, 156
Chillocothe Rocker-stamped pottery 116
chlorite schist 116
Choctaw Indians 134
Chukchi Sea, Siberia 35
chunkey 133, 134
Church Rockshelter No. 1, North Carolina 14, 51–56, 65, 67, 135, 136, 147, 159
Church Rockshelter No. 2, North Carolina 15, 99, 102, 104–107, 135
Civil Works Administration 6
clay figurine 116, 125
clay pipe 116, 137
Clovis, New Mexico 21, 30
Clovis culture 19, 20, 21, 24, 26, 30
Clovis-first hypothesis 20, 29

Clovis projectile point 13, 14, 23, 24, 25, 27, 33, 34, 35, 36
Coe, Joffre L. 6, 7, 60, 62, 73
Cold Canyon site, North Carolina 59, 62, 63, 64, 72–73, 86
Colvard, Fred 32
Colvard II site, North Carolina 32–33
Connestee phase 114, 116, 118, 120, 121, 125
Connestee pottery 114, 115, 116, 117, 119, 120, 122
Connestee projectile point 117
cooking/baking 46, 47, 51, 54, 76, 84, 85, 88, 96, 97, 98, 105, 122, 128, 129, 151
Coontree site, North Carolina 59, 63
copper 9, 86, 93, 109, 110, 111, 116, 122, 124, 148, 154
core and blade technology 26, 27, 28, 116, 122
Coweeta Creek site, North Carolina 145, 146, 147, 150
Cranberry Rock, North Carolina 151
Creek Indians 134
cremation 51, 85, 88, 89, 94, 95
cremation urn 85
crystal quartz 67, 116, 118, 125
Cumberland Plateau 42, 43, 44, 49, 50, 87
cupule 83, 84, 136, 139, 151, 152

dacite 23, 26, 27, 28, 32, 34, 36, 39, 49, 60, 62, 66, 67, 69, 70, 93, 105, 106
Dall, W.H. 20
Dalton projectile point 21, 28, 29, 36
Dan River 151
Dan River phase 132
Dan River pottery 132
dating methods 13–15
daub 140, 150
deer button game 134
Del Rio jasper 105, 116
De Soto, Hernando 3, 4, 148, 154–156
dire wolf 144
Doerschuk site, North Carolina 60, 61, 62
dog 38, 96, 97, 108, 112, 122, 123, 124, 128, 136, 153, 154, 156
dog burial 108
domesticated plants 25, 87, 88, 92, 94, 98, 103, 120, 127, 129, 130, 132, 136, 139, 153, 156
drill 18, 32, 33, 45, 46, 102, 108, 103
drought 24, 127, 130
Dust Cave, Alabama 23, 42, 45, 46, 47, 48, 50, 51, 72, 86
Dutch Creek site, North Carolina 47, 51–55, 159
dye 92

Early Paleoindian period 21, 25–26, 29–32
eastern mud turtle 29
Eastman Rockshelter, Tennessee 88

Index

Ebenezer projectile point 63, 73, 100
egalitarian society 74, 88, 89, 104, 110, 119, 132
electrical resistivity 11
elk 4, 17, 57, 72, 82, 88, 108, 109, 134
Elk Park, North Carolina 155
end/hide scraper 18, 28, 32, 42, 45, 46, 54, 72, 102, 108
Erwin quartzite 89, 93, 105, 106, 108, 148
European trade items 146, 148
Eva site, Tennessee 67, 81
excavation 12–13
exchange 29, 67, 74, 76, 77, 89, 93, 94, 95, 110, 111, 116, 120, 124, 126, 132, 148, 149, 154

Fallam, Robert 156
feasts/feasting 113, 120, 124, 126, 150
fish/fishing 5, 29, 67, 87, 88, 89, 92, 96, 109, 120, 124, 149, 150, 153
flint 17, 19, 21, 23, 26, 27, 70, 116
Flint Ridge chalcedony 116, 124, 125
Flint Run jasper 35
Flint Run Paleoindian Complex 35, 40, 49
flotation 12, 72
Fluted Point tradition 26–35, 44
food storage 8, 98, 108, 141, 142
forest burning 82, 88
forest clearing 83
Fort San Juan 156
fossil shark's teeth 25
French Broad River 5, 98, 113, 121, 126, 132

Garden Creek Mound No. 1, North Carolina 125, 146, 149, 150
Garden Creek Mound No. 2, North Carolina 114, 121, 125–126, 140, 148
Garden Creek site, North Carolina 7, 114, 119, 124–126
Gardner, William S. 31, 35, 40, 44, 49
Gentleman from Elvas 156
geophysics 11, 125
giant ground sloth 17, 23
glottochronology 94, 95
goosefoot 87, 92, 94, 120
gorget 102, 103, 108, 116, 122, 149, 150
graphite 45, 47, 54
Gray Fossil site, Tennessee 9
Great Smoky Mountains 22, 60, 86
Green River 93
Greenland ice core data 24
greenstone 77, 82, 93, 133, 134, 136
Greenville projectile point 26, 101, 108, 109, 110
grid 10
griddle 46
grinding stone 27, 38, 43, 51, 55, 64, 72, 82, 94, 102

grooved axe 77, 79, 82–83, 92, 93
ground penetrating radar 11, 126,
Guaxulle (Guasili) 148, 155, 156
Guilford phase 59, 62–63, 73
Guilford projectile point 62, 63, 67, 73, 74
Gwyn Hayes site, North Carolina 14, 29, 65, 66, 70–72

hammer stone 38, 42, 43, 47, 54, 64, 67, 83, 89, 97, 102, 105, 108, 139
Hardaway projectile point 21, 28, 29, 36
Hardaway site, North Carolina 42
Harrill, Annabel 32
Hatshepsut 160
Hawksbill Mountain, North Carolina 119
hearth 8, 12, 14, 39, 54, 69, 70, 71, 72, 75, 84, 85, 108, 122, 129, 130, 138, 150
hellbender 19, 106
hematite 45, 47, 54, 108
herbaceous annuals 82, 87, 88
Herculaneum, Italy 9
hickory nuts 5, 37, 50, 72, 84, 89, 91, 94, 97, 120
Hidden Valley Rockshelter, Virginia 136
Hiwassee River 152
Hiwassee Rock, North Carolina 152
Holocene Epoch 40, 49, 51, 52, 54, 59, 77, 81, 142
Hopewell 111, 117, 124, 125, 126, 127
Hopewell Interaction Sphere/Phenomenon 111, 117, 125–127
Hopewell Mound Group, Ohio 117
horse 3, 17, 18, 22, 23, 144, 154, 158
horticulture 80, 87, 88, 95, 103, 127, 130, 132
Hypsithermal Climatic Episode 58

Icehouse Bottom site, Tennessee 42, 43, 45, 47, 48, 51, 72, 86, 114, 117, 118
Iddins projectile point 63, 73, 77, 78, 80, 86, 89, 105
Iddins site, Tennessee 77, 86, 88, 91–92
Indian Knoll site, Kentucky 81
Iroquois, Iroquoian 4, 56, 94–95, 133
Israel 19, 24

jack pine 18, 22,
Jack's Reef projectile point 105
jasper 26, 27, 30, 31, 35, 36, 39, 42, 43, 45, 52, 53, 55, 61, 62, 105, 116, 120, 139, 144
Joara 153, 155, 156
Jordan 24
Judaculla Rock, North Carolina 152

Kanawha phase 59
Kanawha projectile point 60, 67
Katie Griffith site, North Carolina 14, 100, 104, 131, 135, 140–142, 145, 149

175

Index

Kennedy, David 11
Kimberly-Clark site, Tennessee 88
King Shalmaneser 20
Kirk corner notched projectile point 34, 40, 42, 54, 55, 56,
Kirk phase 47, 49,
Kirk stemmed phase 59
Kirk stemmed projectile point 59
knife 9, 18, 19, 25, 26, 39, 44, 45, 53, 64, 77, 79, 80, 81, 88, 89, 90, 93, 98, 103, 105, 108
knotweed 51, 103, 120
Knox chert 26, 32, 33, 36, 54, 60, 105, 108, 118
Kotelny Island, Siberia 35

Lake Baikal, Siberia 36
Lake Hole Cave, Tennessee 136, 142–145
Lamar 146–148
Lamoka projectile point 77, 78, 81, 89, 94, 95, 105
L'Anse aux Meadows, Newfoundland 160
Late Middle Archaic phase 59, 63–64, 93
Late Middle Archaic projectile point 64
Late Paleoindian period 21, 23, 27–29, 30
Laurentide ice sheet 21
LeCroy phase 43–44, 51
LeCroy projectile point 40, 41, 43–44
Ledbetter projectile point/knife 77, 78, 79, 81
lithic recycling/scavenging 14, 23, 34, 53, 82, 92, 106
Little Ice Age 4, 142, 145, 154, 156, 157, 158
Little Tennessee River 5, 72, 91, 113, 126, 132, 145
Long Branch pottery 98, 108
Lounsbury, Floyd G. 94
Lovelock Cave, Nevada 9
Lower Kirk corner notched projectile point 40, 41, 42–43, 54
Lower Kirk phase 41 42–43, 54

MacCorkle projectile point 42
Macon County Industrial Park, North Carolina 121
magnetometry 11
Main site, Kentucky 44
maize 103, 120, 127, 129, 130, 132, 136, 139, 153, 154, 156
mano 132, 139,
marine shell artifacts 76, 93, 108, 109, 110, 122, 124, 132, 133, 137, 144, 148, 149, 150
marsh elder 103
Martin, Paul S. 30
mastodon 17, 22, 23, 29
maygrass 87, 103, 120
Meadowcroft Rockshelter, Pennsylvania 20, 21, 25, 26, 29, 30

medicine pipe 102
Medieval Warm climatic period 127, 129, 142, 145
megafauna 21, 23, 29, 30, 40
metáte 51, 132, 139
metavolcanic rock 23, 27
mica 5, 108, 116–117, 118, 121, 122, 124, 125, 126, 137, 148, 149, 151
microblades 116, 122
Mid-Holocene Climatic Optimum 58
Middle Paleoindian period 21, 23, 26–27, 31, 159
migration 17, 18, 20, 21, 23, 29, 30, 32, 38, 39, 49, 52, 66, 69, 72, 86, 87, 89, 93, 94, 104, 113, 114, 140, 142
Miller projectile point 25, 26
Miller II site, North Carolina 67, 68
Mississippian culture 105, 125, 131, 132, 148–152
modified animal jaws 109, 110, 113, 122, 123, 124
mollusk shell 69, 77, 81, 107, 108, 109, 120, 124, 149
Monte Verde site, Chile 20
Moravian 4, 157
Morrow Mountain phase 13, 59, 60, 61–62, 63, 66, 69, 74
Morrow Mountain projectile point 61, 62, 67, 70, 73, 105
mortar 83, 88
mound 5, 6, 7, 8, 20, 77, 111, 112, 113, 114, 116, 117, 118, 119, 120, 121–127, 132, 140, 145, 146, 148–150, 153, 154
mound exploration 5, 6, 7, 20
Mount Rogers rhyolite 62, 66, 93, 105
muskox 21, 22, 29, 31

Naco, Arizona 30
Needham, James 156
net sinker 80, 91
nets/netting 25, 47, 48, 70, 75, 80, 114, 130, 131, 139, 142
New River 8, 17, 18, 29, 32, 33, 70, 113, 115, 135, 140, 151, 156
Newman chert 32
Nikwasi Mound, North Carolina 6, 7
Nolichucky phase 148, 157
Nolichucky projectile point 101, 102, 105, 106, 108, 109, 110, 115
Nolichucky River 107, 108, 148
Norris Reservoir, Tennessee 54
Norse 129, 160
nutting stone 83, 84

offering 107, 119, 137, 144, 149, 150
optically stimulated luminescence (OSL) dating 14, 15, 27, 105
Otarre projectile point/knife 77, 78, 81

176

Index

Ötzi (Iceman) 9
Overhill Cherokee 85

palisade 128, 135, 137, 138, 145, 148, 149, 150
Palmer projectile point 42
Palometta ware 46
Pardo, Juan 156
passenger pigeon 23, 96, 150, 153
Peachtree Mound and Village site, North Carolina 6
peccary 22, 23, 29
pedestrian survey 10
pepo squash 87, 103
pestle 79, 83, 88
petroglyph 83, 151, 152,
Phipps Bend site, Tennessee 107
Piedmont Plateau 22, 23, 27, 30, 32, 39, 42, 58, 59, 60, 61, 62, 66, 69, 73, 84, 93, 113, 132, 157
Pigeon phase 106, 114, 115
Pigeon pottery 106, 115, 125
Pigeon River 113, 118, 125, 149
pigment 45, 54, 122
pigweed 51, 94, 103
Pisgah phase 131, 149, 150, 151
Pisgah pottery 132, 137, 149
Pisgah serrated projectile point 105, 133, 139
pitted cobble 45, 54, 55, 67, 68
plant domestication 25
plant foods/medicine 87, 88, 93, 96, 110, 120, 129, 136, 139
plant remains 8, 12, 72, 73, 91, 107, 109, 120, 121, 122, 139
Pleiades 83–84
Pleistocene Epoch (Ice Age) 21–24, 30, 31, 36, 37, 54, 144
Pleistocene overkill 30
Plum Grove site, Tennessee 145, 148
pokeweed 51
Polynesia 20
Pompeii, Italy 9
porcupine 14, 58, 67, 159
posthole/postmold 108, 125, 137
pottery (ceramic): dating 14–15, 105; disks made of 133, 134; introduction of 40, 77, 98, 103, 104; manufacture of 98
Pre-Clovis 19, 21, 25–26, 29, 32
prepared clay surface 45–46, 48, 51, 72, 86
preservation 2, 8, 9–13, 31, 50, 51, 67, 69, 70, 72, 81, 88, 103, 104, 106, 107, 109, 120, 124, 125, 139
Purrington, Burton L. 7, 106, 115

Qualla phase 145, 146, 148, 151, 157
Qualla pottery 146, 147, 157
quartzite 26, 49, 60, 62, 63, 67, 69, 72, 73, 75, 76, 77, 79, 88, 89, 90, 93, 94, 98, 100, 105, 106, 108

Radford pottery 114
red spruce 18, 22
Redstone projectile point 19, 21, 23, 27
resharpening 53
rhyolite 27, 43, 49, 62, 66, 69, 77, 79, 93, 94, 105, 106
Ritchie, William 40, 77, 78
ritual 5, 77, 97, 107, 113, 118, 120, 122, 123, 124, 125, 126, 130
rockshelter 12, 14, 15, 20, 21, 25, 49, 50, 51, 52, 53, 55, 56, 57, 65, 67, 86, 88, 98, 99, 102, 103, 104–107, 114, 115, 118, 128, 129, 130, 135, 136, 147, 152, 159
Rossville projectile point 94

St. Albans phase 43
St. Albans projectile point 40, 41, 43
St. Albans site, West Virginia 40
Saltville Valley, Virginia 21, 23, 29, 31–32, 156
satellite imagery 11
Savannah River phase 59, 73
Savannah River projectile point/knife 79, 89
seasonality 29, 30, 35, 49, 52, 62, 66, 72, 74, 86, 87, 88, 89, 91, 93, 94, 98, 103, 104, 107, 110, 111, 113, 120, 126, 130, 142, 145, 157, 159
Sergeant Moyano 156
Shady formation 36, 60, 61, 105
shaft-and-chamber burial 137, 150
Shenandoah River/Valley 14, 30, 34–35, 49
Shumate, Scott 72
side-chamber grave 150
Sioux/Siouan 4, 56, 157, 158
Smithsonian Institution 5, 20
soapstone 5, 65, 75–76, 77, 79, 84–85, 91, 92, 93, 94, 95, 98, 102, 103, 111, 116, 130, 133, 142, 146, 152, 160
soapstone vessel 5, 75–76, 77, 79, 84, 85, 91, 92, 93, 94, 95, 98, 102, 103, 111, 160
solstice 118, 119, 123, 125, 126
Solutrean culture 20
Spangenberg, August Gottlieb 4, 157
Spanish 4, 5, 148, 156, 157
Spruce Pine, North Carolina 84
Stanford, Dennis 20
Stanly County, North Carolina 42
Stanly atlatl weight 65, 66
Stanly phase 59–61
Stanly projectile point 59, 60, 62, 67, 69, 70
steatite *see* soapstone
Stillhouse Hollow Cave, North Carolina 130, 135
Stonehenge, England 10, 160
stratified site 10, 12, 13

Index

Stratton Meadows site, North Carolina 86, 91–92
sumpweed 87, 120
sunflower 87, 92, 94, 96, 103
surface survey *see* pedestrian survey
SV-2 site, Virginia 31–32
Swannanoa phase 98
Swannanoa pottery 14, 15, 94, 99, 100
Swannanoa projectile point 63, 73, 94, 100
Swannanoa River 98, 113, 121, 150
symbolism 46, 84, 98, 99, 102, 116, 119, 121, 123, 126, 128, 131, 149, 151, 152
systematic interval testing 10, 32

Table Rock Mountain, North Carolina 119
Tallahassee, Florida 5, 29
Tellico Reservoir, Tennessee 40, 49
Tennessee Archaeological Society 107
Terminal Paleoindian period 28
textile 45, 46, 48, 72, 86
Thomas, Cyrus 20
Thunderbird site, Virginia 24, 30, 31, 34–35
Timberlake, William Henry 85
toad 106, 149, 150, 151
Todd, North Carolina 84, 135, 140
Toe River 92, 148
Townson site, North Carolina 7
trade *see* exchange
Trans-Atlantic migration 20–21
transegalitarian society 104, 120
triangular arrow point 26, 101, 105, 108, 109, 116, 117, 132, 139, 144
Tuckasegee site, North Carolina 7
typological confusion 49, 101
Tyrolean Alps, Italy 9

University of North Carolina, Chapel Hill 7, 114
Upper Kirk corner notched projectile point 40, 41, 42, 43
Upper Kirk phase 43, 51
Uwharrie formation 61, 105, 106

Valle Crucis, North Carolina 52, 67, 80, 104, 159
Valley and Ridge province (VRP) 5, 9, 22, 23, 26, 30, 31, 42, 43, 49, 50, 52, 54, 59, 60, 61, 62, 63, 66, 73, 88, 93, 98, 103, 105, 107, 113, 114, 120, 139, 157
vein quartz 42, 43, 60, 62, 63, 77
village 3, 6, 86, 89, 104, 112, 116, 118, 119, 120, 124, 125, 126, 128, 129, 130, 132, 135–139, 145, 146, 148, 149, 150, 153, 154, 156, 158, 159
Vinette pottery 94

Wagner Island, Tennessee 137
Wakeman II site, North Carolina 89–90
Wakeman III site, North Carolina 117
Ward, Benjamin 137, 158
Ward site, North Carolina 132, 134, 136, 137–139
warfare/conflict 67, 82, 89, 93, 95, 98, 104, 109, 110, 120, 127, 133, 148
Warren Wilson site, North Carolina 7, 79, 98, 103, 110, 114, 115, 137, 145, 150
Watauga Reservoir, Tennessee 137, 142
Watauga River 52, 67, 104, 114, 115, 120, 135, 136, 137, 142, 157, 158
Watts Bar pottery 98, 100, 105–108
West Jefferson, North Carolina 84
white-tailed deer 4, 13, 17, 18, 19, 23, 29, 38, 39, 40, 44, 51, 57, 58, 67, 72, 82, 87, 88, 93, 96, 97, 103, 106, 108, 109, 112, 120, 122, 124, 125, 134, 150
wild grape 51, 88, 91
wild turkey 17, 23, 38, 40, 44, 67, 72, 96, 97, 106, 108, 109, 120, 124, 125, 150
Winklers Meadow Road site, North Carolina 69–70
Wiseman's View Rockshelter, North Carolina 118–119
wolf 18, 19, 113, 122, 123, 124, 144
wooly mammoth 17, 21, 23, 30, 36
world renewal 112, 118, 123, 126

Xinjiang Province, China 9
Xuala (Joara) 3, 154, 155

Yadkin River 4, 5, 17, 61, 70, 126, 132, 148, 157, 158
Yadkin triangular projectile point 101
Younger Dryas climatic event 24, 27, 30, 36, 37

178

www.ingramcontent.com/pod-product-compliance
Ingram Content Group UK Ltd.
Pitfield, Milton Keynes, MK11 3LW, UK
UKHW042014140426
5217IPUK00015B/1173